# THE
# HAPPY NEUROTIC

## The Happy Neurotic

Copyright ©2007 by David Granirer

We acknowledge the financial support of the Government of Canada through the Book Publishing Industry Development Program for our publishing activities.

ISBN: 1-894622-75-8

Published by Warwick Publishing Inc.
161 Frederick Street, Suite 200
Toronto, Ontario M5A 4P3 Canada
www.warwickgp.com

Distributed in the North America by
Client Distribution Services
193 Edwards Drive
Jackson TN 38301
www.cdsbooks.com

Design: Clint Rogerson
Editor: Melinda Tate

# THE
# HAPPY NEUROTIC

## HOW FEAR AND ANGST CAN
## LEAD TO HAPPINESS
## AND SUCCESS

## DAVID GRANIRER

Warwick Publishing
www.warwickgp.com

# TABLE OF CONTENTS

# Section I:
# THE BASICS

CHAPTER

## WHAT IS A HAPPY NEUROTIC

### The Accidental Comic

Welcome to Stand-Up Comedy Clinic. You folks are about to fulfill your lifelong desire to become stand-up comics!

It was just three minutes after class had begun, and already Mavis was plotting her escape. My opening pronouncement was so unexpected that for a moment she was stunned, like a deer in headlights. Mavis had no idea how this mistake could have happened, but she was certain of one thing: this first evening of her new night school course was going to be the last. Of all the things Mavis ever had a lifelong desire to do, stand-up comedy was nowhere on the list. Yet judging by the cheerful laughter and nearly unanimous nodding of heads, she was the lone holdout, surrounded by eager, would-be comedians.

Mavis focused her attention on me, the instructor, as I described the next eight weeks of preparation for the showcase, when each student would have five minutes in the limelight at a local comedy club. Mavis thought about those five minutes, picturing a disastrous scenario: "Hi, I'm a senior who should be at home doing needlepoint, and say, have you heard the one about the retired teacher who wore Depends?"

But as a Happy Neurotic, Mavis knew to use her fear as motivation to analyze her situation. She began a mental inventory. Humor? Yes—

she was all for it. Humor was the reason she was here tonight. She'd heard that I was a stand-up comic but also a counselor and a specialist in using humor to cope with adversity. Mourning her daughter, killed in a skiing accident at age thirty, Mavis had heard about me from her grief therapist. Thinking that my course was on using humor to alleviate grief, she had decided to sign up. Neglecting to read the course description, she had instead wound up in Stand-Up Comedy Clinic.

Certainly Mavis could see the humor in the situation. But the prospect of actually trying to do comedy was terrifying. "I'm much too old for this, and besides, everyone here but me must be naturally funny. If I stay I'll make a fool of myself," she thought. "Seniors don't do this kind of thing, it's undignified and embarrassing." For a moment, Mavis imagined being on that stage, in front of an audience of 200 silent patrons.

That was enough for her. She concluded that once out the door after class, she would find the administration office and withdraw from the course. In the meantime, she would revise her plans for Tuesday evenings. She would be willing to do almost anything, with the sole exception of stand-up comedy.

• • •

But in the end, Mavis did not leave my comedy class, as her growing audience of fans knows. I encouraged her to stay, and she did, but on one condition: "I'll come to class, but I absolutely will not do the showcase." Seven weeks later, Mavis not only did the showcase, she rocked! No one was more surprised than Mavis herself when she became, at age seventy, an accidental stand-up comic.

But getting to the reason I'm telling this tale: Did Mavis have fear and self-doubt? Mavis says they never left her for a second. She felt terrified and insecure during every class. In fact, as far as Mavis is concerned, those uncomfortable feelings were and continue to be the *key to her success,* providing her with an infinite source of motivation.

Mavis has an unusual attitude—the attitude of people I term "Happy Neurotics." What I'm here to tell you is that no matter how much wisdom we acquire, we will never completely rid ourselves of anxiety, fear, and other so-called negative emotions. But as Mavis knows, we can become Happy Neurotics: people who use their negative emotions to create happiness and success *and* have a sense of humor about it all.

## Why the Sense of Humor?

Happy Neurotics know that no matter how much personal growth work they do, how many self-help books they read, or how many workshops they attend, they will never believe in themselves 100 percent, be totally confident, or achieve a state of spiritual oneness. And they don't really care! Rather than berating themselves for not achieving these personal growth ideals, Happy Neurotics use their sense of humor to celebrate their fear-driven and neurotic way of getting things done. They also use humor as a way to cope with adversity. Later in this book I'll give you tools for developing a Happy Neurotic sense of humor, but for now, let's get back to the interesting idea of using negative emotions to create happiness and success.

## Don't Worry, Be Happy

Growing up in North American society, we are constantly reminded that it's flirting with disaster to allow ourselves to experience a negative emotion. This is so ingrained, some of our earliest memories are of ourselves as children being told, "Don't cry, don't worry, don't be afraid, don't be angry, don't be so emotional." It's no wonder that the first response a lot of us have to negative emotions is to try to find an easy, instant way to get rid of them. After all, it's what our parents always told us to do.

Consider the case of John and Linda, a couple I met at a workshop.

Bluntly put, John and Linda's financial situation was a disaster. Both were unemployed and had mountains of debt. On top of that, they had children to clothe and feed. However, this was no reason to panic, or so they were told. The universe would provide if they trusted their higher power and resisted the fear-driven reality of others in their situation. As a matter of fact, their families had just given them a chunk of money to pay down their credit card bills.

But instead of paying debts, the couple used this money to enroll in a series of New Age personal development workshops. Doing so, they believed, proved they were not mired in fear and "scarcity" — just the opposite. These workshops would affirm their belief in "abundance." It was only a matter of time before infinite wealth would flow their way.

They believed they had done the right thing. The workshops were thrilling and the motivational speaker had brilliant insights. John and Linda soon realized for certain that their money difficulties had been emotional, not financial. They had, they were told, created this financial crisis through their negative thinking, and they must now learn to "manifest abundance."

There were others around them who also needed to eliminate negativity. Another participant volunteered that she was afraid to try a risky career change because of the financial insecurity that would result if things didn't go well.

The speaker replied that she was choosing to be afraid, choosing to doubt her own truth, and that she must abandon her scarcity thinking. "After all, what's the worst that could happen? You could go broke. Big deal. Once you've been really poor, you're over it."

The applause swelled. John reached over and squeezed Linda's hand as they both listened raptly to the speaker's instructions: "If you choose to be afraid of financial insecurity, that is just an excuse for not taking control. You will never get anywhere until you release all your doubts and adopt a program of "no-excuses living."

John and Linda were pumped. They were now truly ready to embrace their own magnificence.

The afterglow of the workshops and John and Linda's trust in the universe lasted only a little bit longer than the money they had handed over to the "no-excuses living" folks. To the couples' dismay and confusion, the only thing the universe provided was a barrage of calls from their creditors. Their children, given a choice, probably would have preferred that Mommy and Daddy had lived in fear and paid off the VISA bills instead of going for the quick, easy fix.

## But Fear and Self-Doubt are Bad Things . . . Aren't They?

John and Linda are not alone. In North America, we have declared war on fear, self-doubt, and other so-called negative emotions. If we can only rid ourselves of these negative feelings, countless self-help books and motivational speakers preach, we can all become millionaires and live lives of abundance. It is becoming more and more popular to believe that the only thing standing in the way of unlimited wealth, power, and happiness is our own negativity. Books, magazines, newspapers, web sites, motivational speaking events, and workshops are all touting life strategies based on having a positive attitude. The notion that there is boundless power in positive thinking has reached saturation levels.

This book, however, contains a common-sense message that challenges the growing conviction that we have only our negative thinking to blame if we are unhappy, poor, or powerless. The old adage, "There is nothing to fear but fear itself," has unfortunately come to signify that fear is an enemy to be vanquished. This idea couldn't be further from the truth. So-called negative emotions are not the enemy. In most people they are a natural physiological phenomenon. We have these uncomfortable feelings to ensure our survival and success as human beings. The problem isn't having fear and other negative emotions; it's knowing what to do with them.

There are all kinds of people in the world. Some are naturally pessimistic; others always look on the bright side. Some are over-anxious all the time; others seldom break a sweat. But no matter what the personality, the fact is that positive thinking alone doesn't work. It has no magical power. What's more, despite the seductiveness of the message and the popularity of positive psychology, most of us know, deep down, that looking on the bright side will not miraculously rid us of struggle and adversity.

We know that "trusting the universe to provide" isn't a reliable way to pay the mortgage, so we go to our jobs every day. We realize that for everyone who has a remarkable stroke of luck that rescues them from the brink of financial ruin, there are millions whose belief in the power of positive thinking can't overcome the consequences of spending more than they have—unless VISA agrees to "trust the universe" in lieu of monthly payments. On stage in his act, my comedy student Al Hassam puts it this way:

> I work at a bank verifying information for credit cards. I was talking to one caller and he said, "How do I know you're legit?"
>
> I said, "Look up our number in the phone book and call and ask for me."
>
> He said, "What are you, some kind of comedian?"
>
> I said, 'As a matter of fact I am, and I have a joke for you. Two guys go into a bar. One of them has a VISA card. Guess which one you are?"

## Trust the Universe, but Tie Your Camel

As the Sufi mystic Rumi said, "Trust in Allah and tie your camel." By all means, place your trust in a higher power, pursue personal growth and spirituality if that is your bent, but also take appropriate and sensible precautions to deal with the issues of your life. After all, you have only yourself to blame if your untied camel wanders away, as John and Linda's did.

Believing that negative emotions are the enemy of success is to ignore important aspects of everyday existence. We experience these emotions for a reason, just as we feel pain for a reason: it is a warning that something is wrong. The feeling of fear or pain puts us on alert and lets us know that we should start looking around for the culprit and decide what to do about it. The only exception is if we suffer from anxiety and panic disorders, or other forms of mental illness that grossly magnify our fears. If so, we must seek help in bringing our fears more in line with reality.

Here's an analogy. Several years ago I was walking down the street and tripped and broke my elbow. Now you're probably thinking, "This guy can't even walk down the street without seriously injuring himself, and I'm supposed to take his advice on how to live my life?" Then again, you're the one who was foolish enough to buy my book. Wasn't the nerdy picture on the cover enough of a warning? Besides, you'll never get your money back now, so you may as well shut up and listen. And here's a life lesson for you. To write and market a book, you don't have to be smart. You just need to have to have a big mouth and an insatiable need for attention.

But back to me and my broken elbow. The first thing I did was rush to the nearest emergency ward. I didn't conclude that the excruciating pain I felt was the problem. I didn't try to make the pain go away by thinking beautiful, holistic thoughts like, "I am now whole and healthy and love everything in the universe." Then again, if I had, they probably would have come out more like, "I am now whole and healthy and love everything in the universe . . . except the jerk who tripped me . . . but I realize that even he is a beautiful human being . . . and maybe if I get in my car really quick I'll have a chance to run him over." I also didn't lie on the sidewalk and trust the universe to provide me with a doctor. I also knew I wasn't choosing to be in pain as a way to avoid taking control of my life. I was in pain because I had broken my freakin' elbow, and if I didn't address it quickly, I'd be in pain for a long time to come. I can't imagine going to the emergency ward and having the doctor say, "Your broken elbow has nothing to do with the fact you fell. It's a manifestation of your fear-driven reality. And see that guy over there that got stabbed in the throat? That's his way of telling the world he feels unloved. He created that with his negativity. I'm not even going to bother treating him until he affirms his inner child. Besides, what's the worst that can happen? Once he's bled to death, he'll be over it." Equally ridiculous would be a workshop for people with fractures in which they are told, "You're choosing to be in pain. Those casts you're wearing are just an excuse for not taking control of your life." By the same token, it's just as absurd to tell people on the verge of bankruptcy that fear is their problem. They *should* be terrified at that point! In reality, it's no more sensible to ignore your feelings of fear when faced with a difficult situation, like John and Linda were, than it is to hobble around like a dork without a cast on your broken leg.

The fallacy in New Age thinking about painful emotions is that they will sabotage and bring down terrible "karma" upon your sorry ass. What I'm here to tell you is that in fact, painful emotions are absolutely essential to you. It takes way more energy to suppress these emotions than it does to understand and use them.

As you read this book, you will see how to analyze situations that trigger the emotions. This will allow you to discover the real nature of your "enemy." I provide step-by-step strategies for using the energy that painful emotions *are designed by nature to provide*. These methods will help you to direct your energy for your own benefit as Mavis did, instead of expending it on trying fruitlessly to get rid of negativity. These strategies will help you become a Happy Neurotic: someone who uses negative emotions to create happiness and success *and* has a sense of humor about it all.

## Be Afraid. Be Very, Very Afraid

In their desire to avoid fear, John and Linda signed up for the "trust the universe" message. They convinced themselves to disregard their anxiety about their financial situation and the messages it was giving them. However, their poverty was not due to living in fear. Rather, they crashed and burned financially because they failed to respect their entirely appropriate fear.

Trusting the universe is a very mellow state, like being back in the womb. Unfortunately there's no motivation to get anything done while you're there. John and Linda could have avoided a spectacular financial disaster if they had used their fear constructively to remove the source of their discomfort (their debt), rather than trying to get immediate, temporary relief from the discomfort itself (their fear of debt). If they had remained afraid of bankruptcy, they might have put their family's money onto their credit card debts, created a budget, and curbed their spending. Had they been more worried and fear-driven, they could have taken some important steps towards happiness.

In contrast to John and Linda's not allowing fear to spur them into action, the story of Mavis's comedic success demonstrates that negative emotions are a powerful tool. The key is to understand them, learn how and when to listen to them (and when not to), and to use them to our best advantage. Because she is able to do just this, Mavis is not just a graduate of my class, she is a spectacular success story. She has performed across the country, and has been interviewed on national radio and television. And she's funny. But, she says, there's no escaping her fear and self-doubt; nor does she want to:

> I am constantly with fear. It's what makes me prepare, edit, practice, learn and subsequently perform better. My theory is that people who are successful are constantly questioning their ability and striving to do better. Preparedness gives me the assurance that I can do the task, but fear and self-doubt provide the edge for me to give the best performance I can.

As Mavis knows from her success as a comic, negative feelings can produce great results. However, those results are only possible if we use these emotions as motivation to act, to work hard to keep our nightmare from becoming a reality.

## When the Going Gets Tough, the Tough Get Scared

It truly is amazing what people can accomplish through fear, self-doubt, and other negative emotions. For every success story about someone fearlessly accomplishing his goals, there are ten about fear-driven neurotic wrecks who, because of their fear and insecurity, pulled off amazing feats. Take my Stand-Up Comedy Clinic course. In eight weeks the students go from knowing absolutely nothing about comedy to performing at a comedy club in front of 200 people. And fear is the prime motivator. How do I know? Aside from the fact they tell me, there's the same pattern in every class. In the first three to four weeks people often don't do their homework, which is to go home and write five jokes each week. But once we get to within three weeks of their final showcase, the terror hits, and they start to churn out an incredible amount of good material.

And contrary to a lot of self-help literature that says fear and self-doubt make us unhappy and can lead to negative consequences, my fearful students generally have a wonderful time and achieve great success. Channeling their insecurity and anxiety into their comedy act becomes an exhilarating and self-esteem-building experience. Their fears give them energy, insight, and make them come alive. For me, it's a beautiful sight — a roomful of Happy Neurotics striving together toward a goal.

As a matter of fact, all my efforts to motivate them in positive ways never have the effect I want. I've tried saying things like, "Think of what a great accomplishment this will be." "You can do it, I know you can." "You should be proud that you're taking this risk—you're so courageous." But two weeks to showcase, and people go into overdrive. I've found the best way to motivate the class is to say, "I can see you're afraid, and I think that's great. I'm confident that your fear will motivate you to bring in some killer material next week." Let's face it, trusting the universe to provide is as hopeless a strategy for stand-up comedy as it is for financial management. I can't imagine telling my class, "I'm not going to teach you anything about stand-up comedy. When you're onstage, just trust your higher power to provide you with laughs." Then again, it would be a great way to generate clients for my trauma counseling practice!

## What If My Fears Paralyze Me?

Let's take a minute here to distinguish between what I refer to as being neurotic and what constitutes an anxiety disorder, mental illness, or other condition requiring professional intervention. By "neurotic," I mean the common usage of the word to describe someone who often feels insecure, anxious, and afraid, not the term clinicians use to refer to some of the aforementioned psychiatric disorders. When someone I term "neurotic" experiences so-called negative emotions, he still has a reasonable amount of control over his thoughts, feelings, and behaviors. Though distorted, his thinking still has, for the most part, some basis in reality. So let's say you're going to a party where you don't know anyone, and this makes you very nervous. Though you feel tongue-tied, awkward, and convinced that people won't like you, you are still able to show up and carry on a sufficiently coherent conversation. In this book I would refer to you as neurotic.

Now let's say that just thinking of going into any social situation is so terrifying that it has kept you virtually housebound for years, or sends you into a panic attack. Or let's say that you've built your whole life around finding ways to avoid any contact with people, social situations, or whatever else triggers your anxiety. Or that you see things other people don't see, hear things other people don't hear, believe strangers are out to kill you for no reason, and have repetitive behaviors like hand-washing and counting that you do in an attempt to avoid some dreaded event or situation. If any of this describes you, you may have a psychiatric disorder or mental illness requiring professional help.

One of the main points in this book is that anxiety, fear, and self-doubt are normal and that when managed properly, these feelings can lead to happiness and success, not to mention heightened self-esteem. In other words, by effectively managing our negative emotions we can become Happy Neurotics. However, when people suffer from mental illness, anxiety disorders, or other conditions requiring professional intervention, fears, anxieties, and other negative emotions become huge, overwhelming, and have life-damaging consequences. Often what is needed in these cases is a combination of medication, therapy, emotional support, and life-skills training.

So if you see yourself in these last two paragraphs, in addition to reading this book please go see your family doctor or local mental health team. I suffer from clinical depression, and seeking that sort of help has made a huge difference for me. But whether you have a mental illness, are strictly what I term neurotic, or like me, have the lucky coincidence of being both, this book can teach you how to use your fear, self-doubt, and other negative emotions to kick-start your engine and actually do something about your situation.

# 2

## WHAT'S THE DIFFERENCE BETWEEN A HAPPY NEUROTIC AND A NEUROTIC BASKET CASE?

### What Is a Neurotic Basket Case?

Peter, single and in his forties, just could not understand why dating never seemed to work out. During a date he would feel things were going well, but afterward his date usually declined further contact. And on the rare occasion she did go out with him again, that second date would be the end of it.

Convinced her husband was going to cheat on her, Mary, a client of mine, subjected him to regular interrogations, making him account for every second of his day. She would fire away with questions as to whether he was attracted to any of the women at work, and whether he was planning on sleeping with them. When he said no, she would administer the coup de grace and accuse him of lying. "How can I ever trust you again?" she'd wail. In reality, Mary's husband was loyal and had never behaved in ways justifying her suspicions. But Mary's constant interrogation regularly created crises, and had it continued would probably have killed the relationship.

In chapter one you learned that Happy Neurotics use negative emotions to create happiness and success. They are able to work with their negative feelings and manage them in productive ways that built their self-esteem. In contrast, neurotic basket cases express their fears, insecurities, and other negative emotions through self-defeating behaviors

*25*

that alienate others and undermine their self-esteem. Instead of consciously coping with fears and insecurities, neurotic basket cases revert to unhealthy, unconscious behaviors in attempts to make these feelings go away. They may demand constant attention and reassurance, talking incessantly. They may try even harder to get people to like them, withdraw into angry silences, or take way too much blame for everything that happens around them. They may also worry ceaselessly about their health, interpreting every ache and pain as a sure sign of illness. They may obsess about seemingly irrelevant details, or attempt to control others through guilt. The typical neurotic guilt-trip is aptly summed up by the Jewish mother joke:

> How many Jewish mothers does it take to change a light bulb?
> "Don't bother, I'll just sit here in the dark."

Though neurotic basket cases can take many different forms, perhaps the best known is the character Woody Allen plays in all his movies, who exhibits most, if not all, of the unhealthy behaviors mentioned in above.

It's important to note that whether or not neurotic basket cases are aware of it, fear is the primary emotion underlying their self-defeating behaviors. *Until they become conscious of, accept, and work with their fear,* they will continue to repeat their unhealthy behaviors. So how do people become conscious of, accept and work with their fear?

Peter finally had the good fortune to date someone who told him exactly what she thought of him: "Don't you ever stop talking about yourself? All evening I've had to listen to stories about you and all the things you've done. I can't get a word in edgewise. You don't listen at all. Everything is all about you."

At first, Peter was angry. How dare she accuse him of being self-centered and inattentive? He was just trying to put her at ease with his witty anecdotes. He would have left it at that, except several days later coincidentally he got similar feedback from a friend. To his credit, Peter decided to do some introspection, to, in other words, begin the task of *becoming conscious of his fear.*

## Getting in Touch with Your Inner Neurotic

Peter realized that for him dating provoked tremendous anxiety, and that his way of coping was to talk non-stop to fill up any awkward silences. Obviously he didn't need to be a rocket scientist to figure this out, but he had been in denial of his true feelings of anxiety for so long that even this rather basic insight came as a revelation. Through talking to single friends, he began to understand that dating makes almost everyone nervous. Concluding that his dating anxiety was relatively normal and that he would never be completely free from it, Peter resolved to find better ways to cope. After all, his amusing anecdotes, though fascinating to himself, had been going over like lead balloons. In the end, all they provided was a sure-fire method of contraception. By accepting his anxiety and becoming aware of how he behaved when feeling it, Peter took the first steps to becoming a Happy Neurotic.

You'll notice that Peter didn't seek to explore the issues underlying his dating anxiety. He didn't attempt to determine whether it was caused by hurtful incidents like rejection or abandonment in previous relationships. Instead, he took a solution-oriented approach, identifying a problem and taking corrective action. You may think this approach is superficial and doesn't address the roots of the problem. And you're right. But it worked for Peter. His goal was to find effective ways of coping with dating anxiety and he did. Perhaps at some point he will have to deal with the underlying issues. But at this time he considered the problem to be solved and wasn't interested in doing any deep exploration. And besides, he now had a girlfriend, so he figured he must be doing something right!

Mary's situation was different. The change came when her husband threatened to leave the marriage if she continued to question his fidelity. In a panic, she made an appointment with me, hoping for professional confirmation of her husband's untrustworthiness. Three sessions later Mary began to understand that she was the one with the problem — fear of abandonment. Initially we used a solution-oriented approach, finding better ways of coping with her fear. Though now able to control her obsessive questioning, Mary's fear of abandonment remained just as strong, and began to show itself in other destructive behaviors. She began to constantly criticize and nag her husband, to which he would reply, "If I want that, I can just move back with my parents!" She would also verbally attack him and reject him sexually. Each time she gained control over one unhealthy behavior, another appeared.

For Mary, unlike Peter, a solution-oriented approach was not enough. To have a healthy relationship, she had to defuse her fear of abandonment by addressing the issues underlying it. These included being abandoned by her father at an early age, and having an emotionally abusive mother. All of Mary's mother's time and energy went into relationships with alcoholic, abusive men. This parental abuse and abandonment gave Mary the message that she was unworthy of love. She grew up believing there was something horribly wrong with her, and that anyone she got close to would see her fatal flaw and abandon her. No wonder she had a hard time trusting her husband!

It took several years of therapy, but eventually Mary realized that the abandonment and abuse were not her fault, that there was nothing inherently wrong with her, and that she *was* worthy and deserving of love. This new understanding helped reduce the intensity of her present-day fear of abandonment. You'll notice I say *reduce,* not *eliminate.* Due to her childhood wounds, Mary will probably always have some fear of abandonment. But lessening its force made it easier for Mary to become a Happy Neurotic, someone able to manage her fears in productive ways that built her self-esteem, using the skills contained later in this chapter. And in the end, becoming a Happy Neurotic also saved her marriage.

## How a Neurotic Basket Case Comes To Be

As children, many of us weren't given proper tools to cope with fear. When we were anxious our parents often said, "There's nothing to be afraid of," or "You shouldn't let that bother you." If we persisted, we got feedback like, "Don't let it get to you." "Don't worry about it, everything will work out." "Stop being so emotional." Though perhaps well intended, these messages gave us the sense our feelings were wrong.

Society has also told us in many instances to never let them see us sweat, to be tough, and that only losers get scared. As a result, many of us have done our best to cover up our insecurities, stuffing them down and pretending they don't exist. This strategy helped many of us survive difficult times, and can still come in handy today. For example, stuffing our fear at a job interview makes sense. In this situation, breaking down into uncontrollable weeping, hiding under the interviewer's desk, and sucking your thumb would at best be unproductive, and at worst, self-sabotaging. Besides, you're only supposed to do that *after* you get the job!

But if stuffing is our only strategy for dealing with fear, we never learn to manage and use it productively. Instead, we express it like Peter and Mary, through unhealthy, unconscious behaviors like non-stop talking or obsessive questioning of our partners. As a matter of fact, always stuffing down fear stunts our emotional growth. When we stuff down a feeling, it stays stuck at the age at which we stuffed it down. In other words, if we began stuffing down our fear at age five, as adults we experience, express, and cope with it as a five-year-old would.

And how does a five-year-old cope with fear? When scared, many five-year-olds become incredibly needful of constant attention and reassurance. They may attempt to make the fear disappear by talking incessantly, try even harder to get people to like them, withdraw into angry silence, or take way too much blame for everything happening around them. They may obsess about seemingly irrelevant details or attempt to control others through guilt. They may also have unexplainable aches and pains, which they interpret as signs of illness. In other words, when they're scared, five-year-olds act like neurotic basket cases.

But what's appropriate for a five-year-old seems ridiculous in an adult. We don't mind continually reassuring a five-year-old that everything is okay, but it's irritating to have to do that for a grown-up. Though tiring, we can find it within ourselves to put up with a child's incessant, mindless chatter. But that behavior quickly loses its charm when the person doing it is 46. As Eufemia Fantetti, one of my Stand Up for Mental Health students, says in her act:

I've had to change my coping skills as I get older. When I was a kid, people used to think it was cute when I pulled my dress over my head. Now they just think I'm desperate and needy.

## Four Critical Things Neurotic Basket Cases Never Got

When we were scared as children, we needed four things:

1. We needed someone to help us identify what we were feeling. Emotions reveal themselves as physical sensations in the body. With proper guidance, children learn to interpret these sensations as messages that they are experiencing certain feelings. What to an adult is fear can appear as a stomachache or choking sensation to a child. When parents label the feeling by saying, "You look scared," the child understands that this physical experience doesn't mean he's unwell, it means he's afraid. The reason many neurotic basket cases constantly think they're getting sick is because they never learned that uncomfortable physical sensations are often signs of emotion, not disease.
2. We needed someone to validate our fear by telling us over and over "It's okay to be scared." People who didn't receive this validation go into adulthood feeling ashamed of their fears.
3. We needed someone to help us clarify what we were afraid of. As children we couldn't always connect cause and effect. We needed a parent or caregiver to ask, "What is it that you're scared of?" and then to help us sort it out.
4. We needed our parents or caregivers to help us develop a plan to address our fear or, if appropriate, to take care of the situation for us.

At age three, Billy was afraid to go to sleep at night. After his parents identified and validated his fear, then helped him problem-solve the situation by installing a night-light, Billy was again able to sleep in his room. But more important, he learned what he was feeling and that it was a valid feeling, and he learned why he was feeling it and what to do about it. Repeating this experience over and over in many different situations gave Billy the tools he needed to become a Happy

Neurotic, someone able to accept and work with his fears, and manage them in productive ways that built his self-esteem.

Now if you're one of those lucky people who consistently got this from your parents then you probably don't need this book. However, if you're like the rest of us and come from one of the millions of families which are dysfunctional, you may want to read on.

## How to Grow Your Fears so They Match Your Age

Though it's fun and tempting to blame our parents for the rest of our life, if we want to develop, our task is to help our immature emotions grow up. We accomplish this by giving ourselves the parenting we missed out on. Here's how:

1. First we need to identify what situations in our life evoke fear, insecurity, and anxiety.

2. Next we locate these feelings in our body. What happens in our body when we experience fear? Where in our body do we feel it? Peter's insecurity manifested as a lump in his throat and tightness in his back. Mary experienced anxiety as a pain in her stomach and an ache behind her eyes.

3. Once we've identified and located our fear, we need to validate that it's okay to have it. But here's where it gets tricky. Sometimes just telling ourselves that it's okay to be scared isn't enough to defuse the shame we have of being afraid. In this case it's important to find a support group and/or a therapist who can help us validate our fears. Receiving validation from others helps us to eventually validate and accept ourselves.

4. In the situations where we feel fear, we need to clarify what exactly it is we're scared of. One way to do this is to list either mentally or on paper exactly what we're afraid might happen, no matter how absurd or irrational it seems. Sometimes consciously identifying how ridiculous our fears are helps defuse them. And if not, we go to Step 5.

5. We need to take some sort of action to address our fear. Among other things, action may take the form of doing something about

the situation, acquiring better coping skills, or seeking professional help to deal with abuse or neglect issues that may underlie our fears.

## Catch Your Early Warning Signs Before You Blow It

Bruce, single and in his early 50s, had a problem. He just didn't realize it. At the start of a relationship he would attempt to sweep his partner off her feet, constantly calling, planning a myriad of activities, and trying to move things along as fast as possible. Inevitably his partner would feel uncomfortable and start to back away, at which point Bruce would try even harder. Needless to say, none of his relationships ever got off the ground, and Bruce could never figure out why.

Bruce had a huge fear of rejection but was totally unaware of it. He truly had no idea why he did the things he did. After coming to me for counseling and becoming aware of the problem, Bruce's next step was learning to catch the early warning signs that he was feeling afraid. Early warning signs are subtle and not-so-subtle changes in thinking, mood, and bodily sensations that precede a descent into unhealthy, anxiety-driven behavior.

Spotting these early warning signs is crucial. When we miss them, we can quickly regress as Bruce did into old, mainly unconscious, unhealthy behaviors to cope with our anxiety. Catching these warning signs gave him the opportunity to make new, healthier choices in dealing with his fears. Bruce's early warning signs included repeated thoughts that he must call his partner immediately, difficulty concentrating on his work, irritability, and a stomachache.

## The Three Key Questions for Spotting Early Warning Signs of Anxiety

By asking the following questions, you too can learn to spot your early warning signs. Think of a time when you felt scared or insecure. What were the early warning signs?

1. What happened to your thinking?
2. What happened in your body?
3. What happened to your mood?

## What to Do When You've Caught Your Early Warning Signs

Once you're familiar with and can catch your early warning signs of anxiety, it's time to ask the Three Key Questions for Coping with Anxiety:

1. "What am I anxious about?"
2. "Is there something I need to do or say to defuse my anxiety?"
3. "Is there something I need to accept?"

By asking these questions you isolate the source of your anxiety, and decide on appropriate means of addressing and/or coping with it. But even if you can't isolate the source, you can still decide whether to take some sort of action and/or accept that you are anxious and move on with things.

For example, when Peter, the fellow who never got past a first or second date, asked himself the Three Key Coping Questions while on a date, the conversation in his head looked like this:

1. "What am I anxious about?"
   *"I'm afraid that she won't like me."*
2. "Is there something I need to do or say to defuse my anxiety?"
   *"I need to take a deep breath, slow down, listen to what she's saying, talk less, and it would also help me to admit to her that first dates make me nervous."*
3. "Is there something I need to accept?"
   *"I need to accept that I feel nervous, and that it's okay to feel nervous, and that I won't do this situation perfectly, but I'll get through it."*

In this example, Peter takes responsibility for his anxiety and does as much as possible to cope on his own. Afterward, if he still needs help or feedback, he can get it from appropriate people such as friends, support group members, or a therapist.

## A Better Way to Ask for Supportive Feedback

Question 2 of the Three Key Coping Questions asks, "Is there something I need to do or say to defuse my anxiety?" During or after a given situation, you might conclude you'd like supportive feedback from someone you trust. The important thing is knowing how to ask for it. Asking "Am I okay? Am I a good person? Do you like me?" probably won't get you any useful information. First of all, those are closed questions to which someone can only respond with "Yes" or "No." And unless she's really callous, she'll respond with, "Yes, of course you're a good person," meaning "I feel awkward having to validate your worth as a human being, so I'll just say 'yes' and hope I never have to see you ever, ever again."

Secondly, asking someone to validate your worth gives them way too much power and undermines you. You're basically indicating that whether or not you are an okay person depends on her saying you are. Even if she assures you a million times, all you've done is create a dependency where you continually seek external validation. After a while, the people you seek it from grow tired of giving it. Then you have to find someone new to validate you, until he or she too burns out.

Instead of trying to get someone to validate you as a person, it's much more productive to ask for feedback on your behavior. A question like, "How did I come across at the party last night?" has several advantages over "Am I an okay person?" Firstly, it's much less threatening, since it doesn't put someone in the uncomfortable position of having to judge your worth. "Could you please give me some feedback?" is also an open-ended request that elicits more information than just "Yes" or "No." It gives people a chance to give valuable insights as to how your behavior is perceived by and affects others. Now you have a chance to actually learn something and change your conduct the next time you're in that situation.

The reason for seeking feedback is to learn something about how your behavior affects others. Obviously, different people will have different perceptions, so it helps to talk to more than one person. And just because someone has an opinion doesn't mean she's right. After doing your research, it's still up to you to decide if you agree with the feedback that you've received.

## The Happy Neurotic Success Formula

The skills in this chapter look great on paper. To the rational mind they make a lot of sense, and there can be a tendency to see them as a cure-all. You may be thinking, "Now that I know what to do when I'm frightened or insecure, I can be totally confident in every facet of my life." Well, think again. As a Happy Neurotic you must understand that you will still feel fear and insecurity. That doesn't mean that you're doing something wrong; it just means that you're human and therefore imperfect. You will still screw up, and there will still be times when you regress into old unhealthy behaviors.

Now I'm going to propose a radical idea that runs counter to what you may have read in other self-help books. As a matter of fact, I'm going to contradict what many motivational experts have to say about success and failure. The Happy Neurotic way of avoiding failure is not to set your eyes on the stars, dream big, or set grueling challenges for yourself. In fact, the Happy Neurotic way of avoiding failure is to set your expectations so low that you'll never be disappointed. That way you'll succeed for sure! For Peter that meant *expecting* to be nervous and tongue-tied on a date. So if he even managed to put together one coherent sentence, he was exceeding expectations. And once he managed that, he could set his expectations slightly higher for next time.

Liz, a client of mine, suffered from social isolation. Though quite successful in her job, it had been years since she'd had a friend. All her free time was spent alone, and the more time she spent alone, the harder it was to take even small risks to meet people. So I suggested an experiment. She would attend a local singles event, but instead of having a goal like talking to a certain number of people, we would consider it a smashing success if she could stay for five minutes and leave without talking to anyone. At our next session she reported staying for fifteen minutes and actually striking up a conversation with someone. By setting ridiculously low expectations, over time Liz was able to build on small successes and slowly develop a social network.

## How Happy Neurotics Catastrophize Their Way to Success

Most of us have read those New Age self-help books that tell us not to catastrophize (worry that everything will go wrong), and to visualize only positive results. Well, I'm telling you to forget it. For the Happy Neurotic, catastrophizing is one of the keys to success. It works like this. Before going into an anxiety-provoking situation, you imagine all the worst things that could happen. Then you come up with a plan to deal with each one. Simply knowing you have emergency plans usually helps to reduce your stress level somewhat. It also lets you differentiate the possible from the absurd.

For Peter, some of the worst things that could happen on a blind date were spilling his drink, wetting his pants, or having his wife show up. Just kidding — he wasn't really worried about spilling his drink! But seriously, he really was worried about being tongue-tied, spilling his drink, or wetting his pants. He decided that it was absurd to think he would wet his pants. He then visualized each of the other possibilities and imagined what he would do to cope. He came up with a witty comeback in case he spilled his drink ("Would you like me to spill your drink too?"). He also planned certain things to talk about in case the conversation lagged. And by the way, good topics to chat about on a first date do not include how much you still hate your ex, the size of your alimony payments, and the plan you're developing to have him or her knocked off and buried in your backyard.

But back to Peter's fears. Did any of these things happen to Peter? No. Had they ever happened before? To a certain extent. But running through the scenarios and his solutions to them in his mind made him feel more at ease. Whenever I do a comedy show, I always expect no one to laugh, and have numerous fallback lines in case that happens. Has the worst-case scenario ever come to pass? Yes, though far less often than I initially feared. As a matter of fact, it's the shows where I haven't catastrophized, the shows I've felt most confident about, where things have gone wrong.

## Preparing for Success: A Quick Route to Failure
Early in my comedy career I accepted a gig entertaining a group of volunteer firefighters in a small town on Vancouver Island. Though having never done more than fifteen minutes of comedy, I decided

that I could do the forty-five minutes this gig called for. After all, I was funny, talented, and believed in myself 100 percent. I would win the audience over with my charisma and charm. Using a sure-fire success technique learned from a motivational speaker, I visualized myself onstage accepting a standing ovation. I also repeated the affirmation, "I am a successful comic. I do hundreds of hilarious shows a year," dozens of times a day.

To make a long story short, it was the worst show I've ever done. They hated me. I did about ten minutes without getting a single laugh. With each joke that bombed, my panic increased. Every second seemed like an eternity. There was no way I could stay up there for another thirty-five minutes. To make things worse, drunk audience members began heckling. Some of the kinder comments included, "You suck! Get off the stage, you loser." Anxiety caused my mind to race in an attempt to come up with something, anything, to escape this humiliation. Finally, in desperation I said, "If you think this is easy, you try it." And then I got the idea to challenge my hecklers to come onstage and tell their favorite jokes. Full of liquid courage, they were only too glad to oblige. For the next 35 minutes they regaled the audience with some of the filthiest jokes I had ever heard. The audience loved it.

My brilliant idea didn't completely salvage things. I had bombed, and that was obvious to everyone. On telling the beefy organizer I couldn't take his money for the show, the reply I got was, "That's good, 'cause I wasn't gonna to pay you." I was tempted to add something to the effect of, "It's great to be on the same wavelength with someone as sensitive as yourself," but decided I didn't want to get beaten up.

Though not a perfect solution, bringing up joke tellers from the audience enabled me to get through in a less humiliating fashion. At least people were laughing at something, and temporarily the spotlight was off me. And I credit my fear for giving me the creativity to think of this idea. Reaching the point of desperation seemed to kick my mind into overdrive, allowing it to consider possibilities well off the beaten path, to think out of the box.

Of course not everyone has the same experience of fear. For some people it is paralyzing, and they just go blank, unable to think of anything. But the principle of catastrophizing holds true no matter how you experience fear. By spending time catastrophizing and planning for the worst-case scenario, you minimize the amount of thinking you have to do on the spot. You use the energy fear gives you prior to facing a situation as motivation to carefully prepare for anything.

### How to Use Your Fear as an Unlimited Source of Motivation

After the firefighter gig, I adopted the Happy Neurotic way to prepare for a show. Rather than set myself up to fail by affirming that I am confident and relaxed, I remind myself that I'm insecure and neurotic, and crumble under pressure. I use my terror of failure as motivation to think up all sorts of bizarre things that could happen and prepare for them.

Whether the situation you fear is a first date, a job interview, giving a public presentation, or a confrontation with a friend, these three steps will give you the motivation you need to apply the Happy Neurotic Success Formula. When faced with a difficult situation:

STEP 1: Remind yourself how afraid and insecure you can be.

STEP 2: Imagine how terrible it would feel to blow it. At this point you may even want to visualize your worst-case scenario.

STEP 3: By now you should feel incredibly motivated to prevent Step 2 from happening. Use this energy to apply the Happy Neurotic Success Formula by imagining everything that could possibly go wrong and planning for how you would cope.

# Chapter 3

# WHAT'S THE DIFFERENCE BETWEEN
# A HAPPY NEUROTIC AND A JERK?

## The Jerk Dilemma

Jerks pose an interesting dilemma for Happy Neurotics. Since Happy Neurotics tend to self-doubt, they are often easy prey for jerks, whose tendency is to blame others. To protect themselves, Happy Neurotics need to understand what makes jerks tick, and to acquire the skills necessary to deal with jerk behavior. This information is also very helpful to jerks who want to make the transition to becoming Happy Neurotics.

## But Isn't It Wrong to Label Someone a Jerk?

As a counselor, I'm trained to avoid labeling people. According to some experts, there is no such thing as a jerk. Obviously these experts never met my first boss! According to these experts, people may exhibit difficult behaviors, but that's because they're in pain. So we're not supposed to call people like my ex-boss who freak out and lose it on us "jerks," because it might offend them. My question is this: Aren't these the very people we *want* to offend? But no, we must use neutral or even positive-sounding euphemisms to describe them so that no one's feelings are hurt. And that's a huge loss. The word "jerk" has a nice ring to it. As I say in my act:

I was in this bar, and this biker threatened to beat me up. Well, as a counselor, my mind is a lethal weapon. I'm trained to use superior communication skills in these situations, so I said, "How would it feel to beat me up?" He said, "Great!" and started hitting me. So I let him have it with the skills I learned at an "Assert Yourself Under Pressure Workshop." I said, "You're beating me up and that's not okay." I realized that he'd had a traumatic childhood, and as a counselor it was my duty to treat him with compassion and respect, so the next time he hit me–I shot the jerk!

That last punchline wouldn't work if I said, "And I shot the socioe-conomically-disadvantaged-verbally-challenged-individual-with-the-overly-assertive-personality-traits-that-are-not-his-fault-and-that-I-should-have-understood-since-I'm-a-more-privileged-member-of-society-and-therefore-a-bad-person."

But over the years I've changed my thinking. I believe that adults, unless suffering from some mental illness causing a complete loss of touch with reality, are responsible for their behaviors. Everyone feels angry, sad, or frustrated from time to time, but they have choices in terms of what they do with those feelings. And if someone, for example, exhibits road rage by yelling at another driver for taking too long to make a left turn, and by making racist, sexist, or homophobic remarks, he's acting, quite simply, like a jerk.

## What Is a Jerk?

Bob, a former client, was a jerk. Or lest I sound too judgmental, let's just say he had a lot of jerk-like moments where he thought it was okay to dump his crap on others. And he had lots of good excuses for his behavior. When acting overly harsh and judgmental, he would say, "I'm just speaking my truth." When he yelled at his coworkers it was because he was "just being real" about how he felt. And he was being real—real obnoxious! If anyone disagreed with his confrontational style they were being "overly emotional and manipulative," or "too sensitive."

Bob had other charming tendencies. In a conflict, he never saw himself as part of the problem because he was always right! It was always the other person's fault, and Bob would tell them so, explaining loudly and in great detail why they were to blame. Occasionally Bob would really lose it, berating people for what he saw as their stupidity and intransigence. Then he would act like nothing had happened, and if they brought it up later he would say he didn't know what they were talking about.

Bob didn't realize it, but people were afraid of him. They either avoided him completely or took great pains not to say anything that would antagonize him. Though he had a senior position in a large company, none of his coworkers respected him. He had few personal friends, and his wife had divorced him years ago.

In chapter two, you learned that a neurotic basket case expresses fears, insecurities, and other negative emotions with self-defeating behaviors that alienate and drive others away. A jerk is pretty much the same thing. The main difference is that a neurotic basket case's behavior tends to mainly hurt himself, whereas a jerk also behaves in ways that damage others' self-esteem.

Jerks tend to have major problems managing anger. For many, anger has replaced all of their negative emotions. Instead of feeling fear or sadness, they just get angry and lash out.

Ironically, beneath their aggressive façade, most jerks *are* neurotic basket cases. They just don't know it. This was certainly the case with Bob. As far as he was concerned he was a confident guy, and if others were intimidated by his assuredness, that was their problem. But in reality, the problem was Bob's insecurity and lack of self-awareness.

It was after another relationship crashed and burned that Bob finally decided to get some therapy. This last relationship had ended so badly even he felt something was wrong. At first he wanted me to just give him the answer. After all, he was paying good money for these sessions, and there must be a quick solution to all this. The quick solution took five years.

It was a huge surprise to Bob when he realized that he was insecure. And it was an even bigger surprise to realize that other people had legitimate reasons to not like his behavior. All of a sudden things made sense. When his last girlfriend had kept saying they needed to talk, she had been hoping he would listen to her concerns, not tell her why she was wrong to have them. The reason coworkers never asked him to lunch was not because they were intimidated by his confidence, but because he monopolized the conversation and verbally attacked them. Or to put it another way, they wanted nothing to do with him because he was a jerk!

## How a Jerk Comes To Be

Most of us were never given the tools to cope with anger. Along with all the negative messages we got about fear, many of us grew up in families that stimulated anger but then blocked its release. Either it was too risky for us to get angry, or our anger was met with useful statements like, "Calm down" (Why didn't I think of that?) or, "You're making a big deal out of nothing—stop being so emotional!"

Unfortunately, when anger is blocked, it remains stuck at the age at which it was blocked. Just as the neurotic basket case expresses fear as would a five-year-old (or whatever age he was when he had to stuff down his fear), a jerk expresses and copes with anger like a five-year-old (or whatever age he was when his anger got blocked).

And how does a blocked five-year-old deal with his anger? He rages and throws temper tantrums. He targets smaller weaker people, or vents his fury on defenseless pets. He smashes his toys or breaks others' stuff. As he gets older, he adds passive-aggressive ways of expressing anger to his repertoire. These include giving people the silent treatment, using guilt-inducing tones of voice, promising to do something he has no intention of doing, and/or making cutting remarks then claiming he was just joking.

Society also gives us a dysfunctional message about anger. We are told it's not acceptable and that we should always remain calm and collected. Then we are presented with role models in movies, TV shows, sports, and video games who freak out and beat people up. So the mixed messages tell us we're not supposed to lose it, but if we do it's in fact okay because we're just acting like our heroes.

## Five Critical Things Jerks Never Got

When jerks were angry as children they needed five things to help them understand and deal with this emotion. Though we may or may not ourselves be jerks, as neurotics, chances are good we didn't get these five things either:

1. We needed someone to help us identify what we were feeling.
2. We needed someone to validate our anger and to unconditionally accept us for having it. We needed to hear over and over, "It's okay to be angry."
3. We needed someone to help us clarify what we were angry about.
4. We also needed to be able to get mad at our parents or caregivers. We needed to hear, "It's okay to be angry at Daddy."
5. We needed our parents or caregivers to set boundaries and help us express anger in a healthy way. We needed to hear, "It's okay to be angry but you need to use words, not name-calling kicking or hitting."

Brad, age five, was mad because his mom wouldn't let him have candy before dinner. He began to throw his toys on the floor. His mom said, "You sound angry. It's okay to be angry at Mommy, but it's not okay to throw your toys. You have to use words to tell me what you're angry about." In the end Brad didn't get his candy, but he got something more important. He learned that it was safe to express anger, how to do it in a healthy way, and that disagreeing with some-one didn't mean the end of the world. Consistently receiving these responses while growing up would help Brad immensely when it came to managing anger as an adult.

## Even If You Get Your Way, Being a Jerk Is Bad for Your Self-Esteem

Even if you get your way, expressing anger like a five-year-old under-mines your self-esteem. Each time Bob lost it and berated his coworkers he would feel ashamed of what he had done, although he wasn't sure why. After all, that's what his dad used to do, so it seemed pretty normal.

What Bob didn't realize was that by expressing anger like a child, he was really expressing his powerlessness. If a child has a lollipop and an adult grabs it away, the child often expresses his powerlessness by raging, throwing a temper tantrum, kicking the walls, or yelling, "I hate you!"

By losing it, Bob was just demonstrating that he felt weak and inferior. He might as well have put a sign on his forehead saying, "I'm insecure." Ironically, when a hockey player elbows an opponent in the face, or a basketball coach screams at the referee, sportscasters refer to them as "tough competitors" possessing a "winning attitude." The truth is that in those moments they are just children in adult bodies, telling the world how weak and powerless they feel. Wouldn't it be great if sportscasters knew that? "And there goes Smith, demonstrating his immaturity and lack of impulse control. Wonder what childhood trauma he's acting out?" And after their tantrums, our sports heroes are made to sit in a penalty box or ejected from the game. Kind of the adult equivalent of sending a kid to his room or making him sit in a corner.

But our sports heroes are let off the hook much easier than children. Once sports heroes serve their time, all is forgotten and they are allowed back in the game. If our child were to beat up another kid, we would expect him to apologize and learn other ways of dealing with conflict.

But back to Bob. After a few raging episodes people began to treat him like a jerk, albeit a dangerous one. They avoided and isolated him, which further reduced his self-esteem. I've heard it said that who we are is often what we get reflected back to us from the people in our lives. This was certainly true for Bob. The more people treated him like a jerk, the more he felt like one. And since he was already a jerk, what more did he have to lose by being an even bigger jerk?

## The Right Way To Get Mad

Becoming conscious of the self-destructive nature of being a jerk gave Bob the motivation to grow up and learn to express anger like an adult. His first step was to understand more about the differences between the ways jerks and adults express their anger.

As you just learned, a jerk expresses anger by
- yelling, name-calling, raging, and/or breaking things
- using violence and physical intimidation
- giving the silent treatment
- making a cutting remark, then pretending it was a joke.

A jerk also expresses anger by
- blaming others for how she feels: "My day is ruined and it's all your fault."
- picking a fight over a seemingly trivial incident
- going on the attack when someone tries to discuss an issue
- dominating or turning a discussion into a monologue or tirade
- telling you what you are thinking or feeling, and portraying it in a negative fashion: "You think you're better than me; I know you do."
- using blanket statements like, "You always. . . ." "You never. . . .".

In contrast, an adult expresses anger by
- clearly and directly stating that she's angry and what she's angry about: "I'm angry that you didn't call me when you said you would."
- attacking the problem, not the person: "I'd like to know that that's not going to happen again," rather than "You're a sorry excuse for a human being."
- being willing to listen to the other person's side of things: "If we got our wires crossed, or something happened that I don't know about, I'd be glad to hear about it."
- asking the other person's opinion: "What do you think we should do about this?"

## Recovering Jerks Should Use the Happy Neurotic Success Formula Too

If you're a recovering jerk making the transition from jerk to Happy Neurotic, don't expect any miracles. Just because you've decided to express anger in an adult fashion doesn't mean the people around you will all of a sudden agree with you. As a matter of fact, be prepared for resistance. In general, people don't thank you when you express anger towards them, no matter how justified you are and how skill-fully you do it. It might even get to the point where you think, "I was better off being a Jerk. At least then people were too intimidated to fight back."

As you learned in chapter two, the Happy Neurotic way of dealing with these setbacks is to set your expectations so low that you'll never be disappointed. Expect the worst from people you confront, and expect that you'll get nervous and blow it from time to time. Like Peter in chapter two, when Bob was going from jerk to Happy Neurotic he catastrophized everything that could go wrong in a given situation, sorted out the absurd, and came up with solutions for the possible. The bottom line when expressing anger is not to cause harm, but if you do, to apologize for it. If you feel yourself about to blow up, then get out of the situation and wait until you've cooled down.

## Catching Your Early Warning Signs Before You Blow Up

In chapter two you learned how to catch the early warning signs that you're feeling afraid and why that's so important to do. The same goes for anger. If you catch them before you blow, you have a chance to make a choice to express your anger in a healthy way. These questions should help you catch your early warning signs:

1. What happens to your thinking?
2. What happens in your body?
3. What happens to your mood?

Bob's early warning signs included thinking that people were stupid, imagining himself yelling at them, tightness in his jaw, and a general feeling of resentment. Once you've caught your early warning signs you can use the Three Key Coping Questions as applied to anger.

1. "What am I angry about?"
2. "Is there something I need to do or say to address my anger?"
3. "Is there something I need to accept?"

When Bob asked himself the Three Key Coping Questions after catching his early warning signs, it looked like this:

1. "What am I angry about?"
   *I'm angry because a coworker reminded me of a project deadline I've missed.*
2. "Is there something I need to do or say to to address my anger?"
   *I need to take a deep breath, slow down, and remind myself that she's involved in the project and has a right to inquire about it.*
3. "Is there something I need to accept and move on?"
   *I need to accept that my anger in this situation is disproportionate and that it's up to me to control it.*

Like most of us, Bob needed lots of trial and error before he saw consistent change. Learning to manage and control his anger was slow and tedious. Progress occurred in baby steps, not leaps and bounds. There were no overnight results, and no amazing split-second transformations. Bob never got to a point where he no longer felt anger, nor should he have. But he learned to express anger as an adult, and to remove himself from a situation when he felt close to losing it.

## Jerkbusting Skills for the Happy Neurotic

As I said earlier, since Happy Neurotics tend to self-doubt, they are often easy prey for jerks, whose tendency is to blame others. In these cases, Happy Neurotics need to recognize the tactics jerks use, and have responses necessary to defend themselves. These are supplied below in "How to Protect Yourself from the Top Ten Things Jerks Say and Do." The basic idea here is to respond non-defensively, and set limits against the jerk's unacceptable behavior. Also, since I'm a comic and can't resist, I've included some smart-ass responses you may want to use but shouldn't. Sometimes just allowing yourself to think of a smart-ass response can help release some of your frustration. And as I said before, a Happy Neurotic copes by having a sense of humor.

## How to Protect Yourself from the Top Ten Things Jerks Say and Do

10. Jerk says, "That's a stupid thing to say."

    **Smart-ass response:** *"I'd get into a battle of wits, but I don't want to fight an unarmed man."* This is a common heckler line that will probably get you beaten up. It's no accident that comedy clubs usually have bouncers to protect the comics! Then again, if you figure you have nothing to lose, try this old Don Rickles line: "Hey is that your face or did your neck just throw up?" But if you want to protect yourself in a more assertive, less aggressive way, here's a safer response: *"It's okay to disagree with me, but it's not okay to tell me that what I say is stupid."*

9. Jerk says, "I was just fine until you brought it up."

    **Smart-ass response:** *"I've talked to your psychiatrist, and he says you've never been fine."*

    **Healthier response:** *"I can see this upsets you, and I feel that our relationship/friendship is too important not to discuss it."*

8. Jerk says, "You're way too sensitive and emotional."

    **Smart-ass response:** *"And I see you've just taken your anal retention pill."*

    **Healthier response:** *"I can see that we don't share the same feelings on this. However, I'm entitled to my feelings, and it's not acceptable for you to judge them."*

7. A jerk may make a hurtful remark, then pretend it was a joke, and accuse you of not having a sense of humor: "Don't you have a sense of humor?"

    **Smart-ass response:** *"Only when I hear a joke that's funny."*

    **Healthier response:** *"Maybe that was funny to you, but I find it very hurtful. If we're to continue this conversation it has to be without those kinds of jokes."*

6. Jerk says, "I wouldn't need to yell at you if you didn't keep making me so mad."

    **Smart-ass response:** *"Whoa, if you didn't like what I just said, you're really gonna flip when you find out I maxed out your VISA card."*

    **Healthier response:** *I can see that you're angry, but it's still not okay* *to yell at me.”*

5. A jerk may blame others for how she feels: “My day is ruined and it's all your fault.”

**Smart-ass response:** *“No, your day was ruined when you got up and looked in the mirror.”*

**Healthier response:** *“I can see you're upset, and if you have something specific to talk to me about, I'd be glad to listen.”*

4. A jerk often tells you what you are thinking or feeling, and portrays it in a negative fashion: “You think you're better than me; I know you do.”

**Smart-ass response:** *“Did you get your mind-reading degree off the Internet? 'Cause if you did, I want one too.”*

**Healthier response:** *“If I've done something to offend you, I'd be glad to talk about it, but it's not helpful when you tell me what I'm thinking.”*

3. Jerk uses name-calling: “You're an idiot.”

**Smart-ass response:** *My friends say the same thing. Only they say it about you.”*

**Healthier response:** *“I can see you're upset, but it's not okay to use words like 'idiot' when you refer to me.”*

2. A jerk might throw things, punch walls, hit, or physically threaten another.

**Smart-ass response:** Unfortunately, when there's a chance of violence, or you feel physically threatened, there is no smart-ass response. The best thing you can do is get the heck out of the situation quickly.

**Healthier response:** *“I can see you're angry, but I won't continue this conversation if you do that again.”*

Please note: Sometimes in these situations the jerk will try and make you stay by saying something like, “But you need to stay here and help me work through my feelings.” Don't buy into it. Let the jerk know that he's responsible for his behavior and working through his feelings himself, and then leave if possible.

1. A jerk often picks a fight over something trivial as a way of distracting attention from the real issue.

**Smart-ass response:** *“Hey that's a good one. I'd be glad to put it on* the agenda for next week's fight. We should start selling tickets now."

**Healthier response:** *"I can see you're upset about _____, but I'm not willing to talk about it until we finish dealing with [whatever the real issue is]."*

## Three Strikes and You're Out: Jerkbusting Strategy #2

Often these healthy responses do the trick, but when they don't, you can use the "Three Strikes and You're Out Strategy" to protect yourself from jerk behavior: Jerks get three chances to change their behavior before you disengage. With this strategy, you lessen self-doubt by reassuring yourself you did everything possible before pulling the plug. For example:

**Jerk:** "That's a stupid thing to say." **Strike One**

**Happy Neurotic:** *"It's okay to disagree with me, but it's not okay to tell me that what I say is stupid. I'd be glad to listen to what you have to say without those labels."*

**Jerk:** "Yeah well it *is* stupid." **Strike Two**

**Happy Neurotic:** *"I told you it's not okay to call what I say stupid. If you continue to use words like 'stupid' to describe what I'm saying, then this conversation is over."*

**Jerk:** "What's your problem? Can't you handle me telling the truth? Your idea is the dumbest thing I've ever heard." **Strike Three**

**Happy Neurotic:** *"This conversation is over. Goodbye."* (Hangs up phone or leaves the room.)

## The Happy Neurotic Disclaimer for Dealing with Jerks

A Happy Neurotic realizes there is no perfect way of dealing with jerks. You might do everything right and still come away from a jerk encounter feeling angry, hurt, sad, or anxious. Despite diligently learning the skills in this chapter, you might completely blow it and end up getting stomped on, or lose it yourself and retaliate with jerk-like behavior of your own. You comprehend that dealing with a jerk will never be a piece of cake, or something to be welcomed as a splendid growth opportunity. Dealing with jerks will always be a drag, period.

If you are in relationship with a jerk that refuses to change, these skills may not be the ultimate answer. Think of it like this: Let's say that walking home each day you get assaulted when reaching a certain corner. You decide to learn martial arts, getting to the point where you can effectively defend yourself. But as long as you pass the same corner, you continue to have to fight. Even though you now hold your own, the question becomes, how much longer do you want to keep doing it? At what point do you reassess your route home? The strategies for dealing with jerks are verbal martial arts. Though you can now mount an effective defense, how much longer do you want to keep having to do it? The solution may be to re-evaluate the relationship rather than continuing to rely on your jerkbusting skills.

# THREE DEADLY MYTHS THAT SET HAPPY NEUROTICS UP TO FAIL

# THE MYTH OF PERFECTION

## I'm a New Age Failure

I'm kind of what you would call a "New Age failure." I've been to tons of workshops and read scads of books that were supposed to change my life, but nothing happened—*zip*. Well, I shouldn't say *nothing* happened; things *have* happened, but not the sort of things I had been hoping for.

One book said that if I changed my thinking, I could reverse disease. So I tried it, and now I get sick *before* I eat at McDonald's. Another speaker implied that if I said positive affirmations, my hair would grow back. And it did. It just didn't look so good coming out my ears.

I've tried hard to adopt New Age ways of being in the world. At a seminar on financial abundance, the leader claimed that if I changed my thinking, abundance would flow my way. So now I think it's okay to steal. He also said that money isn't the problem; it's merely a symptom of what goes on underneath. And I agree. My friend is rich, and it's a symptom of the marijuana grow-op in his basement. Finally, the leader promised to reveal the hidden cause of all my financial problems. I replied, "No thanks, I've already seen my kids today."

Yet another book asserted that the reason I have back problems is fear of money. Apparently, all would be well if I affirmed, "Everything I need is taken care of." And it worked. My back pain disappeared the same day they repossessed my house and car!

## But Is It Really All My Fault?

But in all seriousness, I've worked really hard at self-actualization. I've said my affirmations, visualized abundance, aligned myself with my spirit guides, communed with my power animals, meditated, chanted, and danced into the light. And after doing all that, I'm no richer, sexier, healthier, or confident than I was before. I haven't reversed the aging process, achieved inner peace, or found bliss in every moment. As a matter of fact, I'm still as neurotic as ever.

So my question is this: Is it me? Am I the reason that nothing seems to work, or is there a problem with what the workshops and books are telling me? And if it's not just me, could there be others in the same boat?

Recently, I actually heard a speaker claim that I could become a millionaire by loving myself and getting rid of negative thoughts. I tried it. Surprise, surprise—I'm still broke. Is it because I'm still stuck in self-loathing? Is it because I have a poverty complex? Or is it because I have a mortgage, two kids, and a VISA card?

And if it's the latter, why would loving myself help? There are lots of rich people out there with major self-esteem issues—just look at Donald Trump! Maybe the reason I'm not a millionaire isn't that I'm dysfunctional, it's that I'm not dysfunctional enough! Perhaps if I get to the point where I feel even more unworthy I'll compensate by going out and making a few billion dollars.

In that case, the fact I'm not a millionaire could be a *positive* reflection of my mental health. I'm just not driven or obsessed enough to do what it takes to make huge sums of money. And no amount of saying affirmations or loving myself is going to make that kind of money miraculously appear in my life. In which case the problem might not be me, but the myth being propagated by much of New Age thought—the myth of perfection.

## What Is the Myth of Perfection?

During his weekly counseling session, Joe, one of my clients, lamented, "I bumped into my ex and she was holding hands with another guy. I started to sweat, couldn't think of anything to say, and felt totally awkward. But I want to achieve a state of being where something like that doesn't bother me."

As his counselor, I wanted to say, "You *can* achieve a state of being where something like that doesn't bother you. But first you have to have a blood/alcohol level of over .08."

In her session, Stephanie, another client of mine, offered, "My whole office is downsizing, and I'm afraid I'll lose my job. But I have to get past my fear and see this as an opportunity for growth."

Once again I had to bite my tongue. What almost came out was, "The only growth will be in your therapy bill."

Where do we get the idea that someday we will reach the point where we no longer experience fear, anxiety, or other negative emotions? Welcome to the myth of perfection.

The myth of perfection goes like this: If we read enough self-help books and attend enough motivational seminars, we will be able to eliminate negative feelings and thoughts. We will always be spiritually centered and in complete control of what happens inside of us. We will be able to approach any situation with total confidence. Once we achieve this state of being we can have it all: tons of money, an awesome sex life, lots of friends, world travel, and reversal of the aging process. We'll always look great, feel great, and never sweat anything. We'll no longer have just good days, we'll have *great* ones.

This myth forms the basis for a whole industry. According to many motivational speakers and self-help gurus, we can quickly, easily transform our life if we buy their products and services. Their proven methods will turbocharge us for success, helping us to achieve material wealth and spiritual enlightenment—all in just 30 days, or our money cheerfully refunded. We can immediately acquire unstoppable self-confidence and techniques guaranteeing us a lifetime of abundance. If we have anxiety disorders, panic attacks, post-traumatic stress syndrome, or other neuroses, one program costing thousands of dollars promises simple-to-learn techniques for immediately overcoming all our anxieties and fears.

I've come up with another simple-to-learn technique for overcoming anxiety and fear. It's called *denial.* And it's free!

Some of these New Age pitches are just as ridiculous. I saw an ad for a "breakthrough" two-minute treatment that gets rid of bad breath permanently. Another ad promised me easy-to-learn dynamite techniques for becoming a better lover. Unfortunately, I've found that the techniques don't work so well when you have to practice alone. Or is that what they mean by learning to love yourself?

If, like me, you've tried and failed to become this perfect human, it simply means you need to take more seminars and buy more books and CDs—or so the New Age thinking goes. And lucky for us, our favorite motivational guru has designed another level of his or her program that is guaranteed to remove any defects left over from the previous level. If that doesn't work, it means we're sabotaging ourselves. Surprise surprise! They just happen to have a program to deal with that too. And if we call their 1-800 number and register now for this $5,000 seminar, we'll get a free copy of their latest book, *Ha, Gotcha Again!* But hurry, space is limited, and if we procrastinate, it'll cost twice as much at the door.

## How the Myth of Perfection Sets Us Up to Fail

So where does this leave Joe, Stephanie, and the rest of us who just can't seem to achieve unlimited success, unstoppable self-confidence, and total happiness? It leaves us denying our reality as human beings. We can't be happy, let alone Happy Neurotics, if we keep rejecting the truth about ourselves. And the truth is that we're all miserable, insecure, fear-driven, pathetic people, living squalid, wretched lives. Okay, so maybe that's just me. But all joking aside, let me rephrase that in a more politically correct way: The truth is that we all have fears and vulnerabilities. Eliminating these human characteristics is impossible, and trying to do so increases the very fear and anxiety it is supposed to rid us of. Not only do we have anxiety, now we have anxiety about having anxiety, not to mention that we're spending time and money trying to eradicate something that can be used to our advantage. As Mavis says in chapter one, fear and anxiety have been the keys to her success, motivating her to prepare, practice, edit, learn, and subsequently perform better.

## Are We Heroes or Zeroes?

But in this New Age, fear and anxiety are just not cool. Our culture of success-at-any-cost makes it hard to accept our imperfections without feeling like we've failed. Adding to our confusion is the way some personal growth seminars use the "hero's journey" mythology.

At one hero's journey–type workshop I attended, the leader said he'd help us get in touch with our inner warrior. He said, "When people are in touch with their inner warrior, they feel invincible and all-powerful." I was tempted to say, "No, that's when they're on crack."

Derived from ancient lore, the hero's journey has three stages. In stage one, the hero receives some sort of call to action, often in the form of a threat from an evil adversary. In stage two, the hero goes into the darkness, battling orcs, dragons, and other losers of the mythic world. In stage three, he triumphantly re-emerges into the light with newfound wisdom that he insists on sharing with everyone, whether they want it or not. Unfortunately, the hero's newfound wisdom usually doesn't include the ability to monitor the body language of others as their eyes glaze over and they slink towards the door in attempts to escape him.

In many personal growth teachings, this hero's journey is used as a metaphor for the process of confronting our fear and emerging as winners. To enhance this experience, these workshops and books incorporate ancient rituals. No longer plain old working stiffs, we are now wizards and warriors embarking upon epic quests. Indeed our powers are extraordinary. After all, what ancient shaman had the omnipotence of a VISA card and cell phone? What knight of the round table could pause from slaying dragons and mellow out in the Jacuzzi?

These incongruities can make it hard to keep up the hero pretense. It's tough to feel we are truly courageous when we pay big money to go to a luxurious retreat center to play bows and arrows for a week or two. In fact, the rituals we emulate were originally designed to push humans to the limits of physical endurance and mental sanity. (And if I want that I can just take my kids to the shopping mall!)

In ancient cultures, pushing participants to the outer limits of their physical and mental stamina during these rituals created a transformational experience. Once the participant had stared death or near-death in the face, he or she could never be the same. But in today's New Age version, we want, and are often told we can have, a quick, easy, transformational experience without the physical discomfort and risk of driving our psyche to the breaking point. It's a Catch-22: We want and are encouraged to believe in a transformational experience that lets us remain within our comfort zone, whereas real transformation requires that we go far beyond it. Thus we undermine ourselves, playing at being heroes, all the while knowing we're not—nor, if truth be told, would we want to be, if we knew the anguish and struggle it takes to be a true hero.

The transformational experience created by ancient rituals was one in which participants temporarily transcended their ego boundaries and experienced oneness with all of creation. Yet in many of today's workshops, the message is, "Become transformed so you can make tons of money, get the lover of your dreams, and reverse the aging process." In other words, "Take this seminar and you'll be rich, get laid, and look great." Rather than free us from ego desires, these workshops make them into the ultimate goal.

Not that there's anything wrong with wanting money and personal power. It's just less pretentious and time-consuming to pursue those goals without thinking we are doing something noble that will somehow benefit humanity. Dropping these pretensions also eases the discomfort that results from commercializing and commodifying another culture's sacred practices.

## The Happy Neurotic Antidote to the Myth of Perfection

So my advice to you Happy Neurotics who secretly desire wealth and power is to just admit it. When I was writing this chapter, my spirit guide got in touch with me. Other people's guides have exotic names like Raven, or Moonclaw, and used to be healers and shamans. Mine is named Irv Finkelstein, and he used to be an investment banker. But now that he's passed over he's become very spiritual, while still remaining an entrepreneur. He's currently working on a leveraged buy out of Hell on behalf of Wal Mart. Anyhow, Irv has come to be somewhat of a sage in the hereafter, and he's transmitted this poem to help guide you in your quest to become a happier, more spiritually attuned person.

> I'm a New Age sage and seer, and I can make your problems disappear
> To get your woes to just melt away, here's the affirmations you need to say
> I love me, and I come first, I am the center of the universe
> Me, me, me, I take good care, and I think like a millionaire
> I now affirm my prosperity—piles and piles of dollars for me
> There's plenty for all but get mine first I must,
> and leave you losers in the dust

Irv's idea is that instead of trying to be perfect and spiritually balanced, you embrace your petty ego needs. Learn to affirm that insecure, status-seeking part of yourself. Allow it to wallow in crass materialism. As a matter of fact, Irv asked me to plug his new book, *It's All About Me,* that helps you do just that. Irv's thesis is that by acknowledging and truly living your self-centeredness, you're far more likely to be happy. As he puts it: Would you rather be spiritual and miserable, or happy and egocentric? And he should know, because in his realm, he meets many entities who bitterly regret missing out on the chance for self-gratification during their time here on earth. It's really quite tragic. One entity, a former Buddhist monk named Shri Ramakesh, lived a life of extreme abstinence on earth. He spent his time in deep meditation and oneness with all of creation. Now that he's passed over, Shri constantly bemoans the fact he never got to ride a Harley and date a blonde with big boobs.

So by all means, be spiritual. Spend time meditating if you must. But don't lose sight of the things that really matter—that big promotion, that time-share in Florida, that Mercedes SUV. Earlier I implied that Donald Trump might have self-esteem issues. But so what? I bet if you asked him, he would say he was one heck of a happy guy. And if he doesn't have time to meditate, he can pay someone to do it for him! Heck, he can pay a whole auditorium full of people to meditate, dance, chant, and say healing affirmations while he goes out and wallows in self-gratification. And that makes him special, because not many people can do that.

## Pass the Salt, Please . . .

But joking aside, I think the important thing here is not to be in denial about what you truly desire and why you desire it. Maybe you want a new car just because you think it's cool, and not because you've become spiritually attuned to the concept of universal abundance. Maybe you're at a place where having stuff just makes you feel good. I've heard it said that no amount of money can create security because true security comes from within. Well, I don't know about you, but I sure feel a heck of a lot more secure when I've got enough money to pay the bills. And I feel good when I've got a nice place to live and decent clothes to wear. Maybe we should be able to feel just as secure without that stuff, but I've not met anyone that does. The bottom line is that it's very good for our self-esteem to be able to go out into the world and get what we want. And in general, our self-esteem suffers when we're not able to do that.

And don't worry that you'll get carried away and become totally obsessed with material things to the exclusion of all else. Most people have enough awareness to maintain a reasonably healthy balance between their need to get stuff for themselves and their need to have relationships and care about others. In other words, chances are good that you'll be able to find that balance without paying me or any other so-called coach or life expert to tell you how to do it.

The myth of perfection implies that we have to become spiritually evolved and eliminate negativity in order to get what we want and be happy. What I'm saying is, as Happy Neurotics we can get what we want and be happy without becoming spiritually evolved. Chances are that if we do learn how to get what we want, we'll eventually evolve spiritually as part of that process, but that's something that takes a lifetime. So don't worry if you have negative thoughts, insecurities, or material desires. It's okay if you're not perfectly centered and at one with the universe in every moment. You don't have to love yourself unconditionally. All these so-called flaws work in your favor, because they qualify you to be a Happy Neurotic. And the best thing about being a Happy Neurotic is that there's no workshop to take. You're living it right now as you read this book.

## The Phone's Ringing But No One's Home

But let's go back to the hero myth for a moment. Bravely answering the call to action, the protagonist in hero myths always seems confident of attaining victory. The message is that we too should boldly forge into the unknown, confronting whichever demons stand in our way. Anything less is self-sabotage, a betrayal of our greatness. If only we could be so inspired. But the truth is that oftentimes, when the call comes, we don't want to answer it. And why should we? Who in her right mind would want to pick up the phone to receive an invitation to wallow in an emotional swamp for an indefinite period of time? Who would want to spend hours in therapy or inner child workshops, dredging up painful experiences, unless she felt she had absolutely no choice?

Our reluctance isn't something to be ashamed of or a sign we've failed as human beings. Reluctance to commit time, money, and effort to strive for a goal is healthy and makes total sense. As Happy Neurotics, we can view reluctance as another so-called negative emotion to channel in productive ways that create happiness and self-esteem. Instead of berating ourselves for lacking courage, we can use reluctance as motivation to carefully examine our proposed course of action. We can rationally weigh out the pros and cons, and also factor in how we feel about our proposed course of action.

And let's say we don't arrive at a clear decision and decide to take a leap of faith. Whether or not it works out, we can still feel good that we did our homework beforehand.

Conversely, an impulsive choice based on saving $50 by registering in time for an early-bird discount is not something we will feel proud of, especially if the seminar tanks. Failing to use our reluctance as motivation to do our homework and thus making a bad choice just undermines our self-esteem, making it harder to succeed in the long run.

## Why Programming Yourself for Success Doesn't Work

Many self-help gurus claim we can quickly, easily program ourselves for unlimited achievement. By utilizing their revolutionary new techniques that eradicate negative thoughts and replace them with positive ones, total success will be ours.

To begin with, there's nothing new or revolutionary about this approach. Therapists have used it for decades under the heading of "cognitive therapy," which involves becoming aware of and challenging distorted thought patterns that may occur when we are depressed or anxious.

Let's say I have a bad show, and catch myself thinking, "I suck, no one will ever laugh at my jokes again. My comedy career is over." Using cognitive therapy principles, I would challenge these thoughts, asking myself questions like, "How do I know for sure that no one will ever laugh at my jokes again?" Answer: "I don't know for sure." Or "Have I ever had a bad show before and then gone on to have a good one?" Answer: "Yes." After using these questions to expose my distorted thinking, I then replace those thoughts with other more realistic and more positive ones such as: "I just had a bad show, but I've recovered from bad shows (more times than I'd like to admit!) and gone on to have good ones." Or I might tell myself: "I've had bad shows before but none have ended my career. As a matter of fact, after a bad show I'm more motivated than ever to practice, write, and edit my act so that I won't bomb again."

Cognitive therapy is effective for many, though not all. Its efficacy is in combating conditions like depression and low self-esteem that are sometimes caused or exacerbated by distorted thinking. However, no legitimate therapist would ever claim that cognitive therapy leads to quick, easy, unlimited success in all areas of life.

The idea behind programming for success by changing our thinking is simple: We are like software, and to change the way we function all we need to do is to write some new lines of code. It all sounds so simple and logical, and our rational mind loves it.

Earlier in this chapter I scathingly criticized the easy, guaranteed success seminars. But to be fair, I have to acknowledge there is some truth to the software analogy. We sometimes do give ourselves self-defeating or self-limiting messages without realizing it. Understanding what these messages are and replacing them with positive ones can certainly help us approach situations with more confidence and willingness to take risks.

But here the software analogy breaks down. Once we program software to function differently (assuming we do it right), that's it. Software doesn't forget. We don't have to reprogram it 200 times a day for the next three years. But reprogramming our mind often involves years of replacing negative thoughts with positive ones. It's not quick and easy, it's not a magic bullet, and it won't necessarily result in huge successes. It requires tremendous motivation, self-discipline, and patience. Rather than a single quantum leap, it's a process of many baby steps.

Furthermore, software lacks the ability to discern whether something is true or not. If only our mind were that simple. Wanda, a client of mine, had read a book telling her she could overcome her insecurity by repeating the affirmation, "I am a confident, happy person, and I face all situations with total self-assurance." The only problem was that she didn't believe it. The truth was, she still felt insecure, and no amount of telling herself otherwise could change that. As a matter of fact, repeating the affirmation just made Wanda feel stupid. And since this revolutionary new technique that was supposed to work quickly and easily didn't, Wanda felt like there must be something wrong with her.

Though the book had said that repeating positive affirmations would feel strange until she got used to it, for Wanda the strangeness never went away. Eventually she discontinued the affirmations because they just didn't feel right. And Wanda is not alone. For her and others who have suffered wounds to their souls, healing requires more than just substituting positive thoughts for negative ones.

### Why It's Good to Have Self-Limiting Thoughts

Unlimited-success programs usually have a message like, "The sky's the limit! You can achieve anything you want! The only limits you have are those you place on yourself!" In this paradigm, all self-limiting thoughts must be banished as we move towards a glorious and abundant future. Again, we are given a simplistic formula that does not accurately reflect reality.

True, telling ourselves that we can't do something, or that we'll fail can lessen our chances of success. We think, "I'll fail anyhow so why bother trying?" But this is not always the case. For some, setting low expectations and telling themselves they can't do something actually takes the pressure off, enabling them to perform better than if they anticipate unstoppable success.

Furthermore, some self-limiting thoughts are there for a reason, and we ignore them at our peril. After attending a success workshop, Wayne, someone I met during my days as a musician, decided it was time to pursue his dream of becoming a rock and roll singer. His weekly success support group urged him to follow his dream, live his truth, and claim his power. The only problem was that Wayne had no talent and couldn't sing to save his life.

One might argue that if Wayne took music lessons and devoted himself to his art, he could eventually rise to the top of the rock charts. Not likely. No amount of voice and ear training made much of a difference to Wayne's tin ear. Musicians at jam sessions saw him coming and fled. He became a joke on the local rock scene.

Through dogged perseverance, Wayne eventually got to the point where he could get bookings where he played seedy bars, bookings other musicians fondly referred to as "death gigs." Doing death gigs meant Wayne spent lots of time on the road playing to audiences that at worst were angry and drunk, at best indifferent. Better gigs were out of the question. No matter how hard Wayne worked, he could never perform at a level most musicians consider barely adequate. Wayne's rock dream had turned into a nightmare.

Had Wayne listened to his self-limiting thoughts, he might have approached his music dream more realistically, saving himself (and others!) years of torture. But every time he expressed doubts as to his musical capabilities, his success team was there to call him on his self-defeating thought patterns.

In chapter one I quoted Rumi: "Trust in Allah and tie your camel," meaning that although the universe is a wonderful place where miracles happen every day, it is also a place where you'll lose your stuff if you don't watch out. A similar truth applies to our ability to succeed. On one hand, we are capable of amazing accomplishments, while on the other, we all have limitations. For example, the fact that I'll never be an NFL linebacker isn't due to my self-limiting thoughts. It's because I'm five feet eight inches tall, weigh 160 pounds, have floppy ankles, and am a total wimp when it comes to pain. The last time I played football, someone on the other team tried to tackle me, so I gave him the ball and ran the other way. Unfortunately, he was only seven years old. If he had been a teenager, I probably would have given him my wallet too! But all kidding aside, the point is this: To succeed in a given pursuit, we need the right combination of talent and determination. Determination without talent is a recipe for suffering, and self-limiting thoughts protect us from that fate.

### Finding the Self-Limiting Thoughts that Help You Succeed

Our success depends on being able to tell the difference between healthy and unhealthy self-limiting thoughts. Healthy self-limiting thoughts usually have a basis in concrete reality and focus on a given situation. For Wayne, a healthy self-limiting thought would have been, "Every time you tape yourself singing, you sound out of tune, and you don't seem to improve no matter how hard you practice." Unhealthy self-limiting thoughts focus on our value as human beings. They include, "You're a total failure," "No matter what you do, you will always screw things up," and "You'll never amount to anything."

Healthy self-limiting thoughts indicate we must realistically evaluate our chances for success in a given endeavor. Something inside tells us to beware. If we ignore this internal warning mechanism for too long, or attempt to blot it out with positive thinking, the healthy self-limiting thoughts eventually become destructive. They go from "I think you should take a look at this" to "You stupid idiot." Think of this warning mechanism as someone whose job it is to protect us. When we continually ignore or override her, she feels powerless to get through, and expresses her powerlessness by yelling and becoming abusive—anything to try and get our attention. Thus, our positive-thinking techniques can become a form of denial, and can turn healthy caution into a self-esteem problem for which we may need therapy.

## Show Me Someone Who Is Without Fear
## and I'll Show You a Fool

Let's imagine just for a moment that we could, as some self-help gurus assert, rid ourselves of all fears. No matter what happened, we would remain calm and serene. Unfortunately, there's a problem with this: It's a drag to be that heavily medicated.

But seriously, our emotions are like a compass that helps us find our way in this world. When working properly, our emotional compass points us toward situations that make us happy, and away from those causing pain. When our compass is out of whack, we lose our way. If the fear part of our compass is too strong, then we may run from too many situations. In these cases, we must work to reduce our fear so that it is proportionate to our reality. But if we don't have enough fear, we can stumble into all sorts of danger. Among other things, we may often end up in abusive relationships and let others take advantage of us.

At an introductory evening for a seminar on achieving abundance, the speaker kept asserting, "We are all one." Afterwards I asked, "If we are all one, how come I have to pay you?" Without missing a beat he replied, "There is no such thing as money, there is only fear. Why are you afraid to take my workshop?" Translation: "The reason you won't plunk down $1500 to take my workshop has nothing to do with your finances; it's because you're letting fear run your life. If you were truly open to personal transformation, you would put this on your VISA card and trust that the money would manifest itself in time to pay the bill." I left feeling flawed, like I had failed some cosmic test of my worth as a human being.

In retrospect, I'd say that putting down $1500 would have been really stupid, seeing as I didn't have it. In an attempt to get my money, the speaker was telling me to ignore my emotional compass as it tried to pull me away. As children we would dare someone to do something like ring a stranger's doorbell, and if he refused we would taunt him: "You're just a big chicken!" To me, the speaker's response felt the same. If I didn't take his workshop, I was just being "a chicken." I felt manipulated. And yet it was my "chicken" that saved the day. The thought of spending a big chunk of money I didn't have scared me more than being labeled a coward, so I left as quickly as possible.

I also believe that someone truly wise and compassionate would have responded with something like: "I know that $1500 is a lot of money, and it makes total sense that you'd want to think this over. I trust you'll make whatever decision is right for you." For my part, if I could replay the situation over again, when the speaker asked, "Why are you afraid to take my workshop?" I'd respond, "Because I don't have $1500, and I'm afraid to incur that kind of debt right now. That doesn't mean I'm not open to personal transformation; it just means I have a healthy concern about spending money I don't have."

## Nothing Can Bother You Unless You Let It . . . Right?

Another major tenet of the myth of perfection is that nothing outside of ourselves can make us feel a certain way. No matter what happens, something can only get to us if we let it. And if we let it get to us, it means we're doing something wrong. Thus if we have a negative feeling, it's our fault since we allowed ourselves to feel that way.

It all sounds so simple. Nothing can make us feel bad unless we allow it to, and if we choose not to allow anything to make us feel bad, then we'll never feel bad again. Thanks to the nothing-can-bother-you-unless-you-let-it principle, we will be forever immune to painful emotions.

This principle is summed up in various personal growth clichés. At a healing workshop, I tried to express fear that an illness I'd had for over a year wouldn't clear up, and was told that I was "choosing to feel afraid." A friend of mine who was upset about the breakup of a long-term relationship was told by a workshop leader, "You're choosing to hurt yourself over that."

Once again, I want to be fair. There is some truth to the nothing-can-bother-you-unless-you-let-it principle. We can at times overindulge or wallow in negative emotions. We can also give ourselves messages of the "poor me" type that turn us into victims.

But the nothing-can-bother-you-unless-you-let-it principle is based on a misunderstanding of where our power to choose lies. In his book *Man's Search for Meaning,* psychiatrist and concentration camp survivor Viktor Frankl states that everything can be taken from us but one thing: the freedom to choose our response to a given set of circumstances. Choosing how we respond is different from choosing how we feel. Nowhere in his book does Frankl imply that concentration camp life did not cause prisoners to feel hopelessness, despair, fear, and anger. His assertion is that each prisoner alone could choose how he or she responded to these emotions. We cannot always choose how we feel about something, but we can choose what we do in response to that feeling.

If we are seriously injured in a car accident that is not our fault, we may feel anger, despair, and sadness. Being told that we are choosing to feel that way is ridiculous and insulting. Most of us would want to reply, "You try being bed-ridden for six months." No one would think of telling Viktor Frankl, "You're choosing to let concentration camp life get you down."

However, it can be helpful if people help us to focus on where our power to choose lies. Instead of having someone tell us to change the way we feel about something, we need him to ask: "What are you going to do with that feeling?" or "What are you going to do about that situation?"

And here is where our power lies. If we react to our post-car accident feelings of anger, despair, and sadness by drinking, isolating ourselves, and watching 14 hours of TV a day, chances are we will feel worse. Conversely, let's say we cope by seeking physical therapy, watching our diet, enlisting the support of friends and loved ones, and filling our days by reading interesting books. Chances are we will feel more hope, less despair, and less anger, although we may still experience despair and anger to some degree.

## You Can't Slice Water with a Sword

Another flaw in the nothing-can-bother-you-unless-you-let-it principle is that it attempts to address emotions with logic. Emotions have a logic all their own that defies the rational mind. Our rational mind says, "The car accident happened four months ago; you shouldn't still be angry about it. The other driver was blinded by the sun and didn't see you. He didn't do it on purpose, so get over it already." Or, "That abuse happened 25 years ago; you shouldn't still be feeling sad about it." Our emotional side just hears "blah, blah, blah, blah, blah . . ." and feels like we don't have a clue as to what's really going on.

In the Rider tarot card deck, feelings are represented by water, the rational mind by swords. The point being made is that feelings flow like a river, while the rational mind seeks to understand and master reality by analyzing it—in other words, by slicing it into little pieces. But when we use the sword to slice up flowing water, it just continues to flow. All of our best sword strokes have no effect. Using the rationally based nothing-can-bother-you-unless-you-let-it principle to deal with feelings is as futile as using a sword to slice water.

Using the wrong tool to manage the flow of our emotions can be damaging and create shame. If we hear enough times that we shouldn't be feeling a certain emotion, we feel shame around having it. If we feel angry about abuse that happened 25 years ago and believe we shouldn't feel that way, then we feel shame around still being angry. The shame gives us a message: "There's something wrong with you for the way you feel." At this point we often put down the sword, and in desperation replace it with heavy machinery. Rather than just trying to rationalize away our unacceptable feelings, we may try to bulldoze them with drugs, alcohol, sex, food, work, or just good old-fashioned suppression. Think of it as trying to block the flow of a river. Damming it with earth and stones causes it to back up and overflow its banks. It loses its direction and becomes a big muddy swamp. And that's exactly what happens when we block our feelings. They spill out all over the place, becoming toxic marshes that exhaust our efforts to fight through their seemingly endless terrain.

## Using Emotional Logic to Navigate the Swamp

Effectively dealing with emotions requires that we understand emotional logic. And no, the term "emotional logic" is not an oxymoron. It just means that emotions are logical, but not linear. Linear logic is based on the principle of cause and effect. If we feel angry, it's because something happened within the past few days to make us angry. So far so good. This linear logic can help explain many emotional reactions. But what if we're still angry 25 years later? Or what if we have a huge reaction to a situation that seems minor? That doesn't make linear sense, because whatever we're angry about happened too long ago or is too trivial to bother us, right? Wrong!

Fred and Jill, two friends of mine, had dated for six months. One hot sunny afternoon they decided to go for a walk, and Fred commented that Jill would be more comfortable in shorts as opposed to the long pants she was wearing. Jill got extremely upset and told Fred to stop trying to control and sexually objectify her. Her level of emotion would have made linear sense if Fred truly was a controlling guy who used women as sex objects. But nothing was further from the truth. Throughout their relationship, Fred had been supportive and respectful of Jill, yet this was not the first time she had accused him of being controlling and manipulative. Even Jill could not explain her reactions.

For Jill, the answer came in therapy. She made the connection between her controlling, abusive father and her present-day reactions towards Fred. Though Fred's comment about wearing shorts was innocuous, to her emotional mind it symbolized an attempt to control her. Rationally she knew it wasn't, but emotionally she reacted like it was.

In the world of emotions, what connects a feeling to an event is *meaning,* not cause and effect. We react strongly to something if it reminds us of or symbolizes something that has hurt us in the past. Scientists have taught rats to fear things like buzzers and lights by giving them electric shocks when they hear the buzzer or see the light. Rats quickly learn to fear the stimulus even when there is no electric shock, because the buzzer or light now symbolizes pain. Unfortunately, we humans are not much more evolved in this respect. Fred's comments evoked a strong reaction in Jill because they symbolized hurtful things her father had said.

The difference between Jill and a rat, or any human and a rat, lies in her ability to rationalize the situation. This is both a blessing and a curse. Unlike rats, we know there is no electric shock being administered along with the buzzer or light and can reassure ourselves of that fact. But this serves to make our strong emotional reaction all the more mystifying. Even though we *know* something is not harmful, we still *feel* like it is, and so, unable to understand why, we decide that what we feel is wrong. So when we hear the buzzer, bell, or in Jill's case Fred's shorts suggestion, we feel threatened, while at the same time telling ourselves there's no reason to be. To navigate these complex situations, we need to change the way we understand our feelings. Instead of using rational logic, we must use emotional logic. Here are the basic principles:

*The Six Principles of Emotional Logic*
1. Being unable to explain why we feel a certain way signals that we need to abandon linear logic and switch to emotional logic.
2. Our feelings in a given situation make sense, even if we may not initially understand why.
3. If we react disproportionately to a situation, it often means the situation has triggered some hidden wounds.
4. To find our hidden wounds we need to understand what the situation that triggered them symbolizes or reminds us of.
5. Once we locate our hidden wounds, we must work to heal them through methods including, but not limited to, introspection, talking to friends, reading self-help books, attending support groups, or seeking therapy.
6. We will never be completely healed, but we can get close enough.

## Emotional Logic Is Not a Cop-Out
After applying emotional logic, Jill was hugely relieved to realize her feelings made sense. At that point it was very tempting to say to Fred, "I behave this way because I was abused, so it's not my fault." Truly, it was not Jill's fault her father had been abusive. But now she was an adult and thus responsible for her behavior. To save her relationship with Fred, she had to change her behavior towards him and work through her unresolved feelings towards her father.

## Take a Break—It Might Just Save Your Life
According to legend, John Henry was one among many slaves set free

after the Civil War. He went to work on the railroad as a steel driver, spending his days driving holes into rock by hitting thick steel drills or spikes.

One day a salesman showed up at the camp and boasted that his steam-powered machine could outdrill any man. John Henry took the salesman up on his challenge, and a race was organized pitting man against machine. John Henry won, but died shortly thereafter from what some say was exhaustion and others claim was a stroke.

Today we all live the legend of John Henry. However, our foe isn't a steam-powered machine; it's the myth of perfection. We may achieve success in our drive to become better, faster, smarter, younger, more beautiful, and more affluent. But eventually something has to give. Trying too hard to attain perfection will end up harming us. It's no accident that stress-related illnesses and auto-immune disorders are on the rise. In auto-immune disorders, something goes wrong and our immune system attacks us. By striving too hard for perfection, we attack ourselves.

## Another Happy Neurotic Antidote for the Myth of Perfection

Instead of striving for perfection, Happy Neurotics strive for "perfectly okay." "Perfectly okay" means saying, "I may never feel confident and self-assured all the time, but that's perfectly okay." That doesn't mean we stop striving to grow and succeed; it just means that we do it in a realistic way. Rather than thinking we must completely eradicate all our emotional triggers, we're prepared to settle for lessening their intensity and managing them more effectively.

Perfectly okay also means accepting that we will never do a perfect job of being perfectly okay. At times we will still compare ourselves to others, or feel unsatisfied with what we have and want more. We may occasionally feel a stab of jealousy upon hearing of a friend's success or good fortune, or feel threatened by someone who is way better looking or more successful.

Perfectly okay also means working with these negative emotions and channeling them in ways that build our self-esteem. For example, if we feel jealous of a friend, we use that jealousy as motivation to sign him up on Internet porn sites and send pizza to his house at 2:00 a.m. Obviously I'm kidding here. This is a really bad idea because most pizza places have caller ID. Fortunately, Internet porn is still pretty anonymous!

But seriously, if we're jealous of a friend, we use that jealousy as motivation to question if we have a conflict with this friend, if something is missing in our lives, or if an old wound has been triggered. Then we take appropriate action, seeking to resolve the conflict, address any defects in our lives, or heal old wounds. In some cases we may decide that nothing needs to be addressed, resolved, or healed. We may just need to remind ourselves that it is perfectly okay to feel jealous, and do our best to express that jealousy in ways that are honest, yet not destructive of ourselves and/or others.

We also realize that it's perfectly okay if our confidence is shaky, that it's perfectly okay to get upset or stressed from time to time. We accept that there will always be situations in our lives that provoke anger, fear, and insecurity, even if we don't like it. In dealing with these situations we do our best to take responsibility for our behavior and apply healthy coping skills, while at the same time realizing we will make mistakes, get triggered, and blow it from time to time.

# 5

## THE MYTH OF CONTROL

### What Is the Myth of Control?

Sadly, some people believe they chose their dysfunctional parents because there was something they needed to learn. And there was: Next time, let someone smarter make the choice! Not only did they choose their parents, but remember that car accident they had last year? They created that through their negative thinking. And their husband's heart attack happened because he didn't love himself enough. And the people who died in that plane crash? They chose to die in order to "elevate the consciousness of humanity," or because "they had experienced all they came here to learn."

Welcome to the *myth of control,* which takes up where the myth of perfection leaves off. According to the myth of perfection, we can eliminate negative emotions like fear and self-doubt and achieve perfect control over what happens inside of us. The myth of control implies that by achieving perfect control over what happens inside of us, we also achieve control over external events. Positive thoughts and emotions attract positive events, while negative thoughts and emotions attract negative ones. Thus, if something bad happens, we caused it by failing to control our negativity. Either that, or we chose to have tragedy occur because there was something we needed to learn from it. And the answer to it all is that by simply by getting with the positive thinking program, we will be safe from harm. It's gotten so that the all-is-sweetness-and-light folks are terrified of thinking a negative thought because it might give them cancer; they're terrified of expressing anything other than joy in case it screws up their karma and they have to spend their next life as a toadstool.

## Everything Happens for a Reason—Or Does It?

The myth of control is so instilled in our belief systems these days that we almost don't notice it anymore. Everyone hears and uses clichés like, "There are no accidents," "Everything happens for a reason," and "You create your own reality."

Certainly there may be some truth to these beliefs. For example, Cheryl, an employee at an organization for which I did consulting work, was avoided and excluded by her coworkers. And no wonder. She constantly complained, criticized, and talked behind everyone's back. Underneath Cheryl's unhealthy behaviors was a host of negative beliefs about her world. She truly thought all people were untrustworthy, and that sooner or later they would reveal their true colors. Under these convictions lay unresolved pain from childhood abuse at the hands of her alcoholic parents.

Thus we have a causal chain: Cheryl's trust in people was violated at an early age. To protect herself from more pain she unconsciously adopted the belief that all people were not to be trusted. Her attitude could be summed up by the phrase, "You're going to hurt me sooner or later, so I won't let you get close enough to do it." This attitude led her to behave in ways that kept others at bay. Tiring of her ceaseless negativity, they excluded and isolated her. Then Cheryl could say, "See? I knew they'd turn on me," and have another reason to mistrust.

It was true. People rejected Cheryl for a reason. It was no accident. And to a large extent she did create her own reality. Once Cheryl got therapy, healed her wounds and learned to trust, she behaved differently and got a more positive reaction from others. By changing what happened on the inside, Cheryl also changed her external reality. So far so good for the myth of control.

Let's take the myth of control even further. Jim, a client used as a case study in a counseling course I attended, was a trauma survivor. He seemed to attract bad luck. He constantly got into fights, had freak accidents, and kept getting dumped in relationships. But there was a causal chain at work here too. Research shows that some trauma survivors have overactivity and oversensitivity in areas of the brain that trigger their fight or flight survival reactions. In other words, they walk around in a constant state of physiological arousal, thus overreacting to just about everything. Through his lack of impulse-control, Jim created the fights, the accidents, the bad relationships, and many other negative occurrences in his life. An overly aroused physiology can also cause people to focus on general dangers and miss specific ones, sometimes resulting in so-called freak accidents. For example, Jim was so alert to any possible threat of physical attack that he didn't see the drill he'd left on the basement stairs, tripped over it and broke his ankle.

By dealing with his issues in therapy, Jim healed his pain and desensitized his overactive physiology. Like Cheryl, his thinking became more positive, his behavior healthier, and his impulse-control better, and thus the responses he received from the outside world changed. But here the myth of control breaks down. These changes did not render Jim or Cheryl immune from having bad things happen to them. They, like all of us, could still end up in a plane crash or car accident. They could still get sick, be robbed, or have their house burn down. No matter how psychologically healthy they were, how many positive affirmations they said, and how much they trusted the universe, these things did not protect them from the fact that in this imperfect world, bad things can happen for absolutely no reason at all.

## But What About Amazing Coincidences?

For years, Barbara, someone I met at a workshop, struggled to become an actor. She took numerous classes, had private coaching, and attended hundreds of auditions. Occasionally she got a part, but it never led anywhere. Finally, in her late 30s Barbara decided waiting tables while hoping for the big break wasn't getting her anywhere. It was time to do something else.

Barbara took a personal development workshop and learned about the power of positive thinking. Armed with this new information, she embarked on a new path, and got her real estate agent's license. All of a sudden, her world just seemed to open up. Breezing through the exam, she easily, almost effortlessly, established a business. Clients and opportunities kept presenting themselves. It felt like she was finally on the right track.

Like Barbara, many of us have experienced times where everything falls into place. Once we move in the right direction, the path opens. And it's tempting to take all the credit. These are not amazing coincidences, we may tell ourselves, but rather we created these opportunities with the power of our mind. By changing our internal reality, we succeeded in changing our external one. And it's tempting to think that from now on, anytime we want something, all we need do is think positive, visualize our goal, and *voilà*, it will come to pass!

When we embark on the right path, affirm and visualize success, wonderful coincidences can occur. Here the myth of control has some validity. But being able to create a positive reality is not an absolute principle. Just because wonderful coincidences happen once or twice does not make positive thinking a guaranteed formula for success. This state of grace and good fortune is not something that can be packaged and sold. It's untrue to say that by adopting a more positive frame of mind we can always manifest anything we want in the outside world. No matter how much positive thinking he did, Viktor Frankl could not change the brutal reality of Auschwitz. To imply that he could is an insult to him and all other concentration camp survivors. A positive attitude can help us survive but cannot always change our external reality.

Coming from a family of Holocaust survivors, I grew up with what I call "amazing escape stories." These were examples of incredible strokes of luck enabling survivors to stay one step ahead of the Nazis. I eventually concluded that in addition to their resourcefulness and cunning, one thing Holocaust survivors had in common was that at various times, and often more than once, they'd had astonishing luck. Just when things looked hopeless, something or someone would rescue them. The universe kept providing, just in the nick of time.

Does this not prove that whatever we need will miraculously manifest itself if we positively align ourselves with our inner core or higher power? Yes and no. In the case of many Holocaust survivors, astounding events kept them alive. It seems like there was some sort of connection between their will to live and events in the external world. However, those cases are relatively few compared to those of the millions who perished. Among the ones who did not survive were many with an equally strong will to live who didn't get that lucky break. Indeed, Viktor Frankl states that many of those who died had a deep sense of faith, a positive attitude, and went out of their way to help others. In fact, he alleges that many of the most admirable perished, while others who were far less spiritually evolved survived.

When it comes to luck, synchronicity, or grace, all we can do is create a state of being that invites it, but whether it actually shows up is beyond our control. We can align ourselves with our higher purpose, visualize success, and say positive affirmations to lay the groundwork, but there are still no guarantees things will go our way. Or sometimes something wonderful can happen for absolutely no reason at all.

## Positive Thinking or Guilt Trip?

By implying that we can control external reality when we often can't, the myth of control can cause profound damage to our psyches. If bad things only happen because we failed to think positive, then we are to blame. AIDS activist David Lewis once told me that during the 1980s and early 1990s he saw numerous AIDS patients go to their death feeling like failures because they could not overcome their disease through positive thinking. Thanks to New Age thought, they believed that they had chosen to get sick and were dying because they did not love themselves enough. Not only did they have to contend with a slow, often painful death, but also huge feelings of guilt and inadequacy.

For these individuals, the sayings "There are no accidents," "Everything happens for a reason," and "You create your own reality" became guilt trips. More generally, these sayings can come to mean: "Everything bad that happens to you is your fault." We may end up being ashamed to admit we are sick, that we got laid-off, or had a car accident, because obviously these are symbols of our failure as human beings.

To add insult to injury, proponents of the myth of control, though often supposedly inspired by divine love, can be downright condescending when dealing with others' misfortune. "He chose to get sick/injured/laid-off/etc., but he's not at the level of consciousness where he's open to realizing it." "She'll keep being sick/injured/laid-off/etc., until she opens her heart chakra and allows spirit to guide her," are just a few trendy ideas the "spiritually attuned" use to write off lesser-evolved friends and family. What a nice way to say, "That person's misfortune could never happen to me because I'm more together than he is." It boggles the mind to think of applying this logic to Viktor Frankl: "He chose to be in a concentration camp, but if he'd gotten spiritually connected he'd have made a different choice."

To fully see the absurdity in the myth of control, imagine applying it to a poverty-stricken, war-torn country. I can't picture telling a resident of such a nation that his country was invaded because he and his fellow citizens didn't love themselves enough. Equally ludicrous would be to say to him, "That drought that destroyed your crops wouldn't have happened if your people had all said positive affirmations like 'I'm a special person,' and 'I love me the way I am.'"

## Negative, Fear-Driven People who Lead Charmed Lives

If the myth of control were true, then all people with a bad attitude or negative thinking would regularly be stricken with catastrophe. But is this really the case?

My Eastern European grandmother, God rest her soul, was one of the most fear-driven, negative people I've ever met. Here's a typical phone conversation I would have had with her:

ME: "Hi Grandmother, it's David calling."
HER: "Thank you, thank you for remembering zat I am alive. Vy you never call me?"
ME: "But I'm calling you now."
HER: "*Oi,* it doesn't matter. I am old, I suffer, und you don't care."
ME: "Sure I care about you."

HER: "But I don't matter. You, you are ze important vun. I live only for you. Und zis is how you treat me."

ME: "So uh, I was just calling to see how you were."

HER: "Me?"

ME: "Yes, how are you?"

HER: "I vant to die."

ME: "Uh, huh . . ."

HER: "*Ach,* what do you care, you, who tinks only of himself. Vy I even talk to you?"

ME: "Uh, think I should go now, this is getting really depressing."

HER: "Good. Call me tomorrow."

As far as dear old grandmother was concerned, disaster was always about to strike, people were vile and untrustworthy, and there was no point to life other than to suffer. Not a day went by when she didn't miserably bemoan her fate. Though she saw herself as the quintessential victim, my grandmother lived a charmed life. She survived the Holocaust in Eastern Europe, partly through fear, which gave her energy and cunning, and partly because of sheer good luck. Though she had what many New Age writers and motivational speakers call "scarcity thinking," she always had more than enough money. And in spite of her negative attitude, which according to the myth of control should have manifested all sorts of horrendous illnesses and tumors that should have killed her by the time she was 25, she lived in good health and died peacefully at the age of 83.

A friend of mine who is a high-ranking executive in a Fortune 500 company always fears losing his job. As far as he's concerned, he could be fired tomorrow. Convinced his work is inadequate and that everyone around him is smarter, better, and more efficient, my friend is a classic example of what the myth of control labels a self-sabotaging personality. Accordingly, the reality he creates should be full of failure and disaster. Nothing could be further from the truth. He continues to rise in the company, is well liked by colleagues, and is considered a star performer. More important, he considers himself to be happy despite his high levels of fear and anxiety.

## The Myth of Control and Magical Thinking

If we live in an imperfect world where bad and good things can happen for absolutely no reason at all, why do many of us persist in clinging to the myth of control? All we have to do is take a good look around to realize it's not true. Why? Because an illusion of control can become a powerful defense.

To survive psychologically, children use what's called "magical thinking" to convince themselves their world is a safe place. Unconsciously deluding themselves to believe they are responsible for everything, they create the illusion that they have far more control than they actually do. To a child, if her parents divorce, it must be her fault. Thus, if she figures out what she did wrong, she can prevent divorce or similar bad things from ever happening again.

By adopting the myth of control's main tenets that there are no accidents or that everything happens for a reason, we grown-ups, too, delude ourselves into believing we have much greater control than is the case. If something bad happens, it's because we had negative thoughts, and since we can control our thinking, banishing negative thoughts will protect us from more bad things.

In children, magical thinking serves a protective purpose, because if they realize how tiny and vulnerable they actually are, this will overwhelm their small psyches. This kind of thinking also gives them hope. Things may be bad now, but the myth of control leads them to believe that sooner or later they'll figure out what they need to do to make it all better; thus, they can look forward to a time when everything is okay.

But a necessary illusion for a child becomes an unhealthy form of denial for an adult, and can lead to the very negative consequences that the illusion of control attempts to avoid. To illustrate, I'll tell you about Nicole, a meditation teacher I once knew. She believed that surrounding her house with white light and love would be a more effective way to prevent it from being robbed than locking the front door! After three robberies, it was Nicole's seven-year-old daughter who finally suggested that Mommy should try locking the doors. The negative impacts of Nicole's beliefs and behavior were that she not only had her stuff stolen, but also put her daughter in the inappropriate position of having to be the adult in the family. Can you imagine banks taking this approach? "No need to use the vault, those gold bars will be safe if we leave them on the street and surround them with universal love."

Similarly, after years of working at an unsatisfying job, Bruce, someone I met at a networking event, decided it was time for a change. Attending a recruitment evening for a New Age multi-level marketing company convinced him he'd found his destiny. Not only was their product the answer to every disease known to humanity, but the fact that this opportunity came along at precisely the right moment meant he was bound to succeed. After all, he told himself, "everything happens for a reason."

Bruce was pumped. His startup kit came with tapes and CDs explaining that success was his for the taking if he turbo-charged his mind by visualizing a glowing, abundant future and telling himself that he was now a winner. Anything less than total commitment meant he was sabotaging himself. Bruce was so certain of manifesting his dream that he decided, to the applause of his fellow distributors, to quit his job right away and plunge headlong into his bold new future.

In his zeal to become the next multi-level millionaire, Bruce neglected little details like making sure he had money to pay the rent, phone, and electricity. Focusing on these issues would be letting fear gain the upper hand, the very thing that could torpedo his chances of success. Now he was at a place where he trusted that whatever he needed would just come along. After all, the universe was there to support him.

Something did come along: an electricity disconnection notice. No problem. Bruce just put it on his credit card. Same with the phone bill, car insurance, and most of his other living expenses. After all, he was living in a state of abundance and was sure to draw to himself the money he needed. It was out there; all he had to do was tap into the "right energy field." What Bruce didn't want to tap into was the realization that his state of mind was similar to a three-year-old's who, when told the family can't afford another week at Disneyland, says, "But you can just go to the bank and get more money."

In his child-like state of consciousness, Bruce figured all his friends would see what a wonderful opportunity multi-level marketing was, and boost his earnings by immediately becoming distributors under him. Unfortunately, nothing could have been further from the truth. Annoyed by the fact Bruce had become a walking, talking sales pitch, his friends avoided him. Now he was in debt and alone. And when he turned to his group of multi-level marketing distributors for support, all he got were pep talks on the importance of remaining positive.

## What If I Like Hanging On to the Myth of Control?

Let's be honest: There is a downside to replacing the myth of control with the Happy Neurotic viewpoint that we live in an imperfect world, a world where events often occur which are outside of our control. To begin with, we lose the sense of comfort that denial gives. But there's more. Earlier, I stated that the myth of control gives children hope. The same goes for adults. Believing that we can protect ourselves from harm by thinking positively can give us hope that everything will work out for us in the future. Believing that "everything happens for a reason" creates order in our world. All those tragedies we hear about on the news make sense now. And since we understand why they happened, we can make sure nothing like that will happen to us. And if everything happens because we create it, we are no longer the victims of random events—we are powerful creators. If something bad happens to us, we can just uncreate it.

Conversely, it's scary to think that even if we do everything right, something terrible could happen to us for no reason at all. And if random tragedy could strike tomorrow, all of a sudden the future doesn't seem so hopeful. It can seem that by jettisoning the myth of control, we trade hope for fear. But that's because we misunderstand the relationship between hope and fear.

## The Glass Is Half Empty *and* Half Full

In *The Positive Power of Negative Thinking,* author Julie K. Norem states that negative and positive moods are somewhat independent. In other words, we can be happy *and* anxious at the same time. We can have high levels of fear *and* high levels of hope simultaneously. We can approach a job interview or blind date feeling like it's never going to work *and* that something good will result.

Many of us today have learned to perceive fear and hope as opposite ends of a continuum. In this either/or scenario, logic tells us we can only have one of these emotions at a time. Thus, if we feel both hopeful and afraid, one of these feelings must be wrong or non-existent. This linear thinking can cause us to focus too much on one emotion and lose awareness of the other. Prior to that job interview, all we are aware of is fear, when in actual fact, we may also be feeling hope and excitement.

Similarly, we can at the same time feel afraid that some sort of random tragedy could occur, *and* feel hopeful that everything will work out for us in the future. In fact, feeling both these emotions can be to our advantage. The fear gives us motivation to take good care of ourselves and do what we can to prevent misfortune; the hope gives us a sense of positive anticipation that we can use as motivation to achieve our goals. Understanding that we can experience both these feelings simultaneously, and that this is to our benefit, may make it easier to let go of the false hope we find in the myth of control. And by letting go of the myth of control, we can approach life in a far more realistic manner. If something bad happens that is beyond our control, we can confront it directly, without feeling guilty or ashamed that we brought it upon ourselves. And instead of buying another book or taking another workshop that promotes the myth of control, we can put that time and money towards something more productive, like upgrading our education, doing volunteer work, or just going out and having fun.

CHAPTER

# THE MYTH OF EMOTIONAL SELF-SUFFICIENCY

## What Is the Myth of Emotional Self-Sufficiency?

In the old spaghetti western movies, we were supposed to admire the gunslinger hero. He never needed anyone, and his attitude towards life was one of cool detachment. He was the strong, silent type, following his own path, not desiring approval or caring what others thought of him. Men got the message that they should emulate him. Women got the message that this was the man they should marry, walking steadfastly at his side, never burdening him with their fears or concerns. At the movies' end we usually saw the happy couple walk off into the sunset together. Of course, these movies never showed the "happy" couple several years down the road, with the wife bitterly complaining that our hero never talks to her and suggesting that if he wants intimacy, he should go sleep with his horse.

Today, of course, women are also action heroes, and surprise, surprise, they're pretty much like the male ones. Well, really the only difference is that they would have a hard time growing a beard. Other than that, our women action heroes also don't have emotional needs. The only difference is that their men don't complain about it!

These stereotypes form the basis for the myth of emotional self-sufficiency. Essentially, it says that we, like our heroes, can and should achieve a state of being where we never look to others to meet our emotional needs. As a matter of fact, just having these needs is a sign we are weak and deficient.

The myth has also been perpetuated by many personal growth philosophies. According to these teachings, we should be complete and whole within ourselves. Until we achieve this state of being, we are not ready to have healthy relationships. We should continue to work on ourselves by attending more workshops, reading more self-help books, saying more affirmations, until one day we are ready to emerge as complete humans. In the meantime, we should become our own "date," and take ourselves out for romantic candlelit dinners and long walks on the beach. (But hey, if we're going to date ourselves, let's inject some realism into the process. In addition to the romance, we should also stand ourselves up every so often, make ourselves pay for everything, and then decide we only like ourselves as a "friend.")

Believing we can meet all of our emotional needs makes life so neat and tidy: No more counting on others. No more worry about being rejected. When we've become so whole and complete, we simply won't need anyone else. Armed with our newfound sense of wholeness, no one can ever hurt us again. It's all so simple.

Or is it? The truth of the matter is, we all have the need to be loved and accepted for who we are and the need to feel that we belong somewhere. How we are supposed to meet these needs without looking to others is, quite frankly, baffling. Personally, I've found that staring at myself in the mirror and saying "I love you" just isn't the same as hearing it from another person, and besides, it really freaks out the other guys in the men's washroom!

But let's not throw the baby out with the bath water. Like the myths in chapters four and five, there is a grain of truth to the myth of emotional self-sufficiency. Looking to others to meet *all* our emotional needs is a recipe for failure. To function in the world, we must be able to meet some of these needs ourselves.

But we can't do it all on our own. In my counseling practice, the clients I find most challenging are those who are socially isolated. Acquiring and mastering the skills to resolve conflict and assert feelings can only occur in relationship to others. Learning healthy ways to channel so-called negative emotions cannot happen in a vacuum.

When there is no one around to trigger us, give feedback, notice our progress, and encourage us, change can come to a standstill.

## Why Loneliness Is a Good Thing

Loneliness tells us our emotional needs aren't being met. The problem many people face isn't feeling lonely; it's not feeling lonely *enough.* In chapter one you met John and Linda who, instead of using money from their family to pay off debts, used it to take personal growth seminars. Had they not drowned out their fear of poverty with New Age thought, they would have probably used this money to pay their bills. Similarly, drowning out loneliness with Band-Aid solutions like New Age affirmations, drugs, or workaholism robs us of the motivation to go out and make friends. Often our pain has to be at a high enough level that we're willing to take risks and make changes. And when we use our pain (in this case loneliness) as motivation to go out and meet new people, we build self-esteem. We take small risks, have some successes and failures, but eventually most of us build a social network. As our network grows, so does our confidence.

Suppressing feelings of loneliness can create a sense of powerlessness that undermines our self-esteem. It's hard to feel good about ourselves when we know something is missing in our lives and we don't do anything about it. Now we have unmet emotional needs *and* a sense of inadequacy arising from lack of action. We feel lonely, then think, "I'm so pathetic for not doing anything about this, no one would want to be my friend." The more pathetic we feel, the less willing we are to risk meeting new people, and thus our loneliness increases. We become caught in a vicious circle, where any motivation derived from the increased loneliness is countered by our dropping self-esteem.

## Heroes and Emotional Black Holes

Many of us never got the tools to identify and meet our emotional needs in healthy ways. Add to that the extreme examples of how to deal with our needs that many of us have seen in our lives or out in the world, and it's easy to see why many of us would go along with the myth of not having emotional needs. The role modeling we received could often be wildly inconsistent. On one hand, there was the strong, silent hero, while on the other, there was the "emotional black hole" character that we may have encountered in our daily lives. The emotional black hole was the complete antithesis of the hero, someone with a seemingly unquenchable thirst for approval and validation. When encountering this person, no matter what we did or said to try to be there for him or her, he or she continued to suck the life force out of us until we were depleted and exhausted. A conversation that should have been over in five minutes could last for hours. It may have felt like we were being drawn into a huge void that could never be filled. Attempts to break free from the emotional black hole's mighty gravitational pull would often be met with guilt trips like, "I thought I could count on you." "So you're just going to leave me now." "It's easy for you to go on your merry way, you don't have my problems." "No one cares about me," and my personal favorite "The only person you care about is yourself." Drained by the emotional black holes' endless needs, overcome by their highly effective guilt trips, many of us would succumb, allowing them to sap our emotional resources until they let us escape.

Given that for many of us the extremes that we had witnessed were the strong, silent hero or the emotional black hole, is it any wonder we chose to identify with the former and eliminate any characteristics reminiscent of the latter? Sublimating our needs seemed far preferable to becoming emotional vacuum cleaners. How could we see emotional needs as healthy when our experience of them with the emotional black hole characters was so negative?

### Why the Myth of Emotional Self-Sufficiency Is Such a Killer

When I was single and in my 30s, I had a strong desire to be in a relationship. I felt lonely and unfulfilled and wanted to start a family. But from attending personal development workshops, I had learned that I should downgrade my *need* for a relationship to a *want*. I should be open to a relationship but completely content and happy without one. Until achieving this state of wholeness, I wasn't ready to be with anyone.

It all sounded so practical. The only problem was, it didn't work. As a matter of fact, I now had two problems. I was still single *and* I felt ashamed of wanting a relationship. I'd also learned that the universe would only provide if I loved myself, and my dissatisfaction with my current situation meant I was failing at that. So I pretended I didn't want something I actually wanted in order to improve my chances of getting it, which made me feel even more desperate. And as we all know, desperation is such an attractive quality! Then again, it's one of the basic requirements for Internet dating.

The reason the "downgrade your need for a relationship to a want and be perfectly content without one" shtick didn't work is that, as you learned in chapter four, you can't slice water with a sword. My need for a relationship was emotional, and the "downgrade your need to a want" shtick was logical. Rationally, it made sense that by changing my programming from needing to merely wanting a relationship, my feelings of loneliness and emptiness would dissipate. Unfortunately, the lonely, empty part of me wasn't buying it. No matter what I told myself, the truth was that I had a strong need for a relationship.

## The Roommate from Hell

When suppressing or denying a healthy human need or emotion, we often end up expressing it unconsciously and destructively. Think of it this way: Let's say we share a small apartment with a roommate. Our roommate wants to discuss certain issues, but we ignore him. Sooner or later, he gets tired of politely asking to have a chat. He gets angry and says, "I'm going to screw up your life until you pay attention to me." He starts partying, playing loud music at two in the morning, eating all our food, leaving the sink full of dishes, and stealing our stuff. He does his best to destroy all our personal relationships so he can have our undivided attention. He also embarrasses us in public with inappropriate displays of anger and insecurity.

Our emotions and emotional needs are our roommates. We can ignore them, but they're not going anywhere. They will persist until we pay attention to them and find healthy ways of addressing them. The more we deny them, the stronger and more vocal they become. Eventually they can take over our being, causing us to act in unhealthy and self-defeating ways. We may sometimes find ourselves losing control of our behavior and not understanding why. For example, denying feelings of loneliness can cause them to intensify and unconsciously influence the way we think and behave. When friends talk about their great relationships, we may surprise ourselves by feeling and behaving irritably towards them. Then again, happy couples can be annoying at the best of times. They should have the decency to be miserable like the rest of us. And here's another sign that we may not be addressing our loneliness: While a good friend talks about having relationship difficulties, we suddenly feel an inexplicable sense of joy, try our best to persuade him to leave his partner, and then make plans to hit on her ourselves. And don't tell me I'm the only one who's ever considered it! But in all seriousness, until we address our loneliness and channel it in ways that build self-esteem (in this case using it as motivation to go out and meet people), chances are good these behaviors will continue.

And if we try and kill our emotional needs, we kill ourselves. Giving up on our need for love and companionship means giving up on life. Life-affirming emotions like joy, love, and hope are often by-products of our connection to others. It's hard to feel hopeful and upbeat when plagued by social isolation. It's hard to want to get out of bed in the morning when it feels like no one cares if we live or die.

Isolation also affects us physically. In *Emotional Intelligence: Why It Can Matter More Than IQ*, author Daniel Goleman quotes research concluding that social isolation is as significant a factor in mortality rates as smoking, high blood pressure, obesity, and lack of physical exercise. This data suggests you're actually better off being a smoker with lots of friends than a socially isolated health food fanatic. Go figure!

### Non-Attachment or Denial?

Emotional needs are often inconvenient. They're messy, awkward, and meeting them takes lots of time and energy. So we find all sorts of ways to circumvent them. Various seminars I took promoted principles from Eastern mysticism. I'd been told that to achieve enlightenment, I should adopt the practice of "non-attachment." This meant that I should not desire things or people. I should live perfectly in the moment, not allowing my ego to trick me into wanting anyone's love or approval. As one seminar leader put it, "We are all one, and to desire is to live in separation from the eternal source of love." All I could think was, "After being stuck in a room with you for the past two days, separation is starting to look pretty good." And wasn't she surprised when I inquired, "If we're all one, how come you desire $600 from me for this seminar?" And if this sounds similar to the "If we are all one, why do I have to pay you?" incident I describe in chapter four, it's because I've taken to regularly asking this question of seminar leaders who preach the "we are all one" thing. Or perhaps it is the universe working through me. Either that or I derive a perverse pleasure from having spiritually evolved beings kick me out of their workshops. In this case, the response I received was, "Money is just a form of energy that allows me to do my sacred work." I was tempted to reply, "If it's energy you need, why not stick your finger in a light socket?"

## Do They Walk the Walk or Just Talk the Talk?

I decided that either she was nuts or I was. So rather than trust the universe, I decided to be neurotic and skeptical. One by one, I reviewed my personal growth experiences with speakers who preached emotional self-sufficiency and non-attachment. Though many had taught it, none seemed to live that way. One Buddhist guru I encountered had sexually harassed female devotees, and another seminar leader had slept with several young female followers despite the fact he was married. Yet another treated his followers with contempt unless they were wealthy and willing to fund his retreat center. Obviously, these individuals had strong attachments to sex, money, approval, and material things. Explanations that their behavior was motivated by "spirit" struck me as pathetic. Though evangelizing against the evils of the ego, these gurus seemed quite happy to wallow in ego gratification.

Of all the participants I had met at the emotional self-sufficiency and non-attachment workshops, none seemed able to live life according to these principles. These included both the beginners and advanced, those who had "graduated" and gone on to "assist" the leaders in running the workshops—for free of course, or sometimes even paying for this privilege. Just as in any other group, there was jealousy and conflict. Cliques formed and people felt left out. Some left the fold, claiming they felt unsupported. Those who stayed accused those who left of choosing to live in separation, egocentricity, or whatever the leaders' buzzwords were to describe people doing it "wrong."

Maybe somewhere out there is someone who meets all his emotional needs himself, and has no attachment to money, possessions, or people, but I have yet to meet this person.

## How Do Happy Neurotics Meet Their Emotional Needs?

Based on the evidence I had collected, I decided that living a life of emotional self-sufficiency and non-attachment was impossible, at least for me. The problem was not having emotional needs; the problem was being told these needs were wrong. The question for me, and indeed for most of us, becomes how to acknowledge and meet our emotional needs without allowing them to turn us into emotional black holes.

To begin with, as Happy Neurotics we must accept that we will never completely meet all our emotional needs. Our job is to get close enough. To do this, we must understand to what degree our emotional needs result from wounds created by abuse or neglect and to what degree they are just healthy human needs.

In chapter two you met Mary, whose unwarranted questioning of her husband's fidelity almost ruined her marriage. Mary had an emotional need for reassurance that she was loved and valued, which in general is normal and human. Her problem was the *amount* of reassurance she needed. Though we all need it at times, Mary needed it all the time. Her disproportionate need for reassurance resulted from unhealed childhood wounds. Her father had abandoned the family when Mary was quite young, while her alcoholic mother had been verbally abusive, often leaving her alone for long periods of time. This wounded Mary so deeply that as an adult she still had an immense fear of abandonment.

Mary's job was not to eliminate her need for love and reassurance, but to heal the wounded part of her that could never get enough. This involved several years of therapy during which she worked through her pain and anger. And no, not everyone needs therapy to heal the wounded parts of themselves. There is no one-size-fits-all remedy. I refer to therapy a lot in this book because it's the form of treatment I'm most familiar with. However, I've seen people heal by, among other things, contemplating their lives, reading books, seeking support from friends, attending healing circles and sweat lodges, meditating, going skydiving, or even taking a comedy course! In one way or another, they have found methods to address painful events in their lives, and make changes in how they behave and think.

But back to Mary: Even after her therapy, Mary was never completely whole. But she was close enough. Now that her wounds were at least partially healed and not so overwhelming, she was able to get them met them in ways that built her self-esteem. Instead of obsessively questioning her husband, she could admit to him and to herself that she was feeling insecure, and ask for a hug. She learned to catch her early warning signs and use the Three Key Questions mentioned in chapter two to help her deal with fear in a healthier way. At times she was able to accept that she felt insecure, comfort herself, and get on with her day, or just get on with her day despite feeling insecure. And sometimes, like all Happy Neurotics, she blew it, regressing back into old destructive behaviors. Though these occasions were never easy or fun, Mary persevered, and over time they decreased in both frequency and duration.

## How Do I Know If My Needs Are Healthy Enough?

A Happy Neurotic knows there is no such thing as "perfectly healthy," but there is healthy *enough*. Like Mary, we all have the need for companionship, support, love, and acceptance. And like Mary, it's a question of degrees. In general, our needs are healthy if we can meet them and get them met by others in ways that enhance our self-image. There may still be times we feel lonely or insecure, but we are able to cope. And each time we are able to comfort ourselves and get on with things despite feeling insecure or appropriately seek support, we feel better about ourselves.

If our needs are overly strong and unhealthy, then satisfying them in healthy ways can be difficult to impossible. We may use things like drugs, alcohol, food, sex, or work to distract us from and numb our loneliness. Unhealthy needs can also manifest in other ways. We may need constant reassurance, be unable to spend time alone, or rarely state what's on our mind for fear of rejection. We may put others' needs ahead of our own, consciously or unconsciously reasoning that if we do so they will like and need us. Since our self-image is so poor, we are often attracted to or stay in friendships and relationships where people treat us disrespectfully. And each time we perpetuate these self-destructive behaviors, our self-esteem decreases.

If our emotional needs are unhealthy, chances are that we suffered a wound to our soul at some time in our lives. To get our needs to the point of being healthy enough, we, like Mary, must address this wound through whatever works for us—therapy, support groups, workshops, self-help books, and the like. Our work is to heal some of the damage, while also learning new coping skills. Once some of the pain heals and its intensity subsides, we can then cope with our loneliness in the Happy Neurotic fashion by channeling it in ways that build self-esteem—in this case using it as motivation to go out and meet people.

## Old-Fashioned Tough Guys, New Age Fascists, and Depression

Another facet of the myth of emotional self-sufficiency involves what I call the "old-fashioned tough guy" attitude towards depression. Depression sufferers are often given the message that they should be able to just get over it, pull up their socks, and stop feeling it—all on their own. It's all in their heads, and if they think positive, it will just disappear. Thus, if they remain depressed, it is their own fault because they are choosing to be negative. Either that or they are weak-willed and defective.

Depression sufferers are also subject to judgements by people I term "New Age Fascists." New Age Fascists think that everyone should be able to overcome depression naturally by changing diet, taking vitamin supplements, seeing a naturopath, meditating, and drinking wheat grass juice. Now I've tried drinking wheat grass juice each morning, and quite frankly, I'd rather be suicidally depressed! According to New Age Fascists, anti-depressants are bad since they just mask the symptoms and induce a false sense of euphoria, allowing people to avoid their issues. New Age Fascists also think that anti-depressants are horrendously addictive and will eventually kill you. And let me tell you, if the anti-depressants don't kill you, being preached at by New Age Fascists definitely will! Finally, they believe that taking anti-depressants means an individual is weak-willed and took the easy way out, instead of being strong and doing things the holistic way. With their view that everything holistic is good, and everything that involves medication is bad, New Age Fascists are as closed-minded in their thinking as some of the medical professionals they despise.

Let's sort through these messages. Old-fashioned tough guys have a point: Depression sufferers do sometimes behave in self-destructive ways that worsen or perpetuate their condition. Overcoming depression is not easy and does require that we be tough, doing things like getting out of bed, getting exercise, and going to therapy. even when we don't want to.

New Age Fascists also make some sense. Some depression sufferers find complementary medicine and lifestyle changes extremely helpful in making them feel better. And in some cases anti-depressants are overprescribed, do have bad side effects, and don't work.

But both schools of thought preach a form of emotional self-sufficiency that can be crippling. Just as most of us can't overcome loneliness on our own and must turn to others, many depression sufferers can't overcome depression without the help of medication. Just as loneliness tells us we lack companionship, depression is often a sign our brain doesn't produce enough neurotransmitters. Without companionship our loneliness will never dissipate, and without these crucial neurotransmitters neither will our depression. It would be ridiculous for a therapist to tell a client, "It's wrong for you to overcome your loneliness by seeking companionship from others. That's just being weak. You should be able to be correct your loneliness through meditation and colon therapy." Equally laughable is to tell a depression sufferer, "You must cure your lack of serotonin by looking in the mirror 50 times a day and saying 'I love you' to your reflection."

Some complementary health practitioners would argue that meditation, changing diet, and taking supplements boosts serotonin levels. And certainly some people have found that healthy lifestyle changes seem to eliminate or reduce depression. However, in my experience, anti-depressants have a high success rate.

Both old-fashioned tough guys and New Age Fascists fail to understand the difference between clinical depression and emotional issues. Though both can overlap, clinical depression is an illness. Think of it like diabetes. In some cases diabetes patients can overcome their condition through diet and lifestyle changes. In more severe cases they must take insulin. We wouldn't think to tell this latter group that they should just get over their diabetes and stop taking insulin. We wouldn't say to them, "You've got to overcome that insulin addiction." Instead, we would support them in continuing to take their medication and in making healthy changes in lifestyle and diet.

I began my counseling career as a New Age Fascist. But much as I hate to admit it, over the years I have seen too many people (other than pharmaceutical company shareholders) profit from taking anti-depressants. And I'm one of those people. Being on the right anti-depressant has made a huge difference in my life. I also notice that once my clients have the chemical imbalance taken care of, they make more rapid and consistent gains in therapy. As opposed to experiencing euphoria, clients on medication tell me, "For the first time in years I feel normal." They still have all their feelings and issues to deal with but now have more energy and resilience.

True, anti-depressants don't work for everyone. Some people can't tolerate the side effects, or they report feeling drugged. And some have to try three or four kinds before they find the right one. This trial-and-error process can take months and, to put it bluntly, can be a real drag.

As Happy Neurotics we channel our so-called negative emotions in ways that build self-esteem. If we feel depressed, we use our depression as we would our fear or our loneliness—as motivation to make changes and address issues. We begin by addressing our issues on our own through methods such as introspection, therapy, and healthy lifestyle changes. Even if taking these steps does not eliminate our depression, the fact that we've taken them helps maintain our self-esteem. Few things are more self-destructive than knowing we have a problem and not dealing with it.

And if we suspect that, in addition to having emotional issues, we also suffer from a chemical imbalance, we use this suspicion as motivation to explore other avenues of treatment, including taking medication.

# EMBARRASSMENT AND SKEPTICISM: A HAPPY NEUROTIC'S BEST FRIENDS

# 7

## IF I'M ON THE PATH TO A HIGHER CONSCIOUSNESS, HOW COME I FEEL LIKE SUCH AN IDIOT?

### You *Should* Feel Like an Idiot When They Ask You to Say "I Love You" to a Pillow!

I once attended a seminar where they put on some mood music and made us say, "I love you" to a pillow. I don't know what was worse, having to say "I love you" to a pillow or having to suffer through the facilitator's choice of music—Julio Iglesias singing the sappiest love songs ever written. But apparently, this process was supposed to create powerful changes. And it did. To this day, just the sound of Julio's voice is enough to traumatize me for days!

But according to our facilitator, this process would help heal our emotional pain. So here we were, a roomful of adults, doing our best to sob and hug pillows. Quite frankly, I felt like an idiot. But when I tried to say something to that effect, I was told my embarrassment was a "manifestation of my self-loathing." If I refused to continue, it obviously meant I wasn't willing to love myself. In hindsight, I realize it just meant I wasn't willing to look like a dork. But there I sat, sheepishly hugging a pillow to prove to this group of strangers that I was open to self-love.

And after we declared our love to a pillow, there was more fun in store for us. We had to go around the room and hug everyone and say to them, "You're lovable just the way you are." Now, I hate hugging strangers. When the first person, a chunky guy in sweat pants that showed off his butt crack, came up to reassure me I was lovable, it was all I could do to restrain myself from replying with, "You freak, get away from me!"

At another seminar, the speaker dimmed the lights, gave everyone a candle, told us to walk around a room of 200 people we hardly knew, and look deeply into their eyes while holding their hands. While we were doing this she made us repeat over and over, "I am enough." The only thought going through my mind was, "I've had enough!"

If you've done some sort of personal growth work, chances are you've been invited to do touchy-feely stuff. And sometimes, when the right atmosphere is created, it can lead to powerful changes. But all too often, these exercises feel like a sloppy invasion of our boundaries. And in these cases, it is natural and healthy to feel embarrassment. What is inappropriate is being told this feeling is wrong.

## Why Feeling Embarrassment Can Be a Good Thing

Embarrassment has two functions. First of all, it protects us from situations that leave us vulnerable and exposed and that can undermine our self-esteem. The message our embarrassment gives us is that we need to either get away from the situation causing it, or to proceed with caution.

Embarrassment also tells us when we behave inappropriately, thus protecting us from saying or doing things that can damage others and ourselves. It's our psyche's way of telling us, "Slow down and think through what you've just done or are about to do." Unfortunately, embarrassment is highly uncomfortable, and we often go to great lengths to avoid it. But as anyone who has been drunk knows, obliterating this emotion often leaves us with huge regrets the next day, especially when we wake up in a cell and realize that our new best friend is a guy named Bubba.

In some personal growth circles, it has become fashionable to idealize children: "They're so spontaneous and expressive. We should all strive to be like that." Small children *are* spontaneous and expressive, because they haven't yet developed the capacity to feel embarrassed.

Imagine for a moment that we too were like that. What would stop us from coming to work naked, eating with our hands, or telling our boss we think he's a poohead? Small children don't need a well-developed capacity to feel embarrassment, because it *is* age-appropriate to run around the house naked and from time to time pee their pants. As adults, thanks to our more advanced ability to feel embarrassment, we hope we have evolved beyond that point.

## Sometimes a Cigar Is Just a Cigar

Admonished by a student for smoking 20 cigars a day, Sigmund Freud replied, "Sometimes a cigar is just a cigar." The student had suggested that Freud's cigar smoking symbolized feeding from his mother's breast. With his response, Freud made the point that some things just are what they are, that not everything has deep symbolic meaning.

Then again, Freud was a weird guy. It certainly seems there was a lot more symbolism going on in his life than he was willing to own up to. Be that as it may, his point is valid. Some things are exactly what they appear to be. Sometimes our feelings in a given situation (like my feelings in the pillow-hugging seminar) are exactly what they are, and not symbolic of deep unresolved conflicts or hidden attempts at self-sabotage.

In chapter four I discussed emotional logic. When operating in this realm of our being, we react strongly to something if it reminds us of or symbolizes something that has in the past hurt us emotionally or physically. However, emotional logic only applies when we react disproportionately to a situation. Regular logic based on direct cause and effect applies when our emotional reactions are in proportion to whatever triggered them.

For example, in chapter four, Jill reacted to Fred's suggestion that she'd be more comfortable in shorts versus long pants by accusing him of controlling and sexually objectifying her. Since Fred had treated her with respect during the course of their relationship, Jill's reaction was clearly disproportionate. When she realized that Fred's comments evoked a strong reaction because they reminded her of hurtful things her father had said, it all made sense to her. Score one point for emotional logic.

However, not all emotional reactions are disproportionate. Had Fred truly been a controlling jerk, Jill's reaction would have been exactly what it appeared to be, an expression of anger towards someone behaving in ways that undermined her self-esteem. In other words, it would have been completely proportionate to the situation. Similarly, feeling embarrassed is a proportionate reaction when we are asked to disclose deep, innermost secrets to a group of total strangers, or to look in the mirror and say "I love you" to ourselves. It's normal to feel stupid if we're told to adopt a mythic name, beat drums, and run around naked in the woods. In cases like this, our embarrassment is not symbolic of hidden self-loathing or anger at our parents. It is a healthy reaction to requests that render us vulnerable, and exposed and that can undermine our self-esteem. In other words, we're *supposed* to feel like idiots when asked to do something weird and unnatural.

## Take the Path of Most Resistance

When embarrassed, we tend to resist doing more of whatever it is that causes our embarrassment. According to some therapists and self-help gurus, resistance is the nemesis of inner growth because it supposedly stops us from getting in touch with and healing our emotions.

WORKSHOP LEADER: "You're in resistance."
PARTICIPANT: "No I'm not."
WORKSHOP LEADER: "Yes you are."
PARTICIPANT: "Am not."
WORKSHOP LEADER: "Are too."
PARTICIPANT: "Am not."
WORKSHOP LEADER: "Are too."

This humorous imaginary conversation highlights the difficulty in determining who's resisting whom. But seriously, in all fairness, it would probably never happen in this fashion. A more realistic version would probably look something like this:

WORKSHOP LEADER: "You're in resistance."

**Translation:** *"I'm getting angry because you won't hug a teddy bear and cry like everyone else at this workshop."*

PARTICIPANT: "I just can't seem to connect with this on a feeling level."

**Translation:** *"Hugging a teddy bear and crying is a stupid idea."*

WORKSHOP LEADER: "Sounds like you're blocked at some deep level of your being."

**Translation:** *"You're not trying hard enough."*

PARTICIPANT: "Yeah, maybe I am, but I just can't seem to get past it."

**Translation:** *"F*** off and leave me alone."*

WORKSHOP LEADER: "This exercise is the key to healing your wounds. I'd like to support you in working through this block."

**Translation:** *"Hurry up and get with the program. Everyone else is already finished and ready to debrief."*

PARTICIPANT: "I'm just not ready to do this."

**Translation:** *"What part of 'F*** off' did you not understand?"*

WORKSHOP LEADER: "I'd really like to support you where you're at. Perhaps you and I could share on the break."

**Translation:** *"It's obvious that you're wrong, but I can't spend any more time with you or the group will think there's a problem. I'll let you off the hook now, but you'd better be ready for the next exercise where you're going to nurture your inner child by curling into the fetal position and sucking your thumb. And by the way, I've cashed your check, so a refund is out of the question."*

To heal our wounds, some personal-growth gurus suggest we must have cathartic experiences. We should beat pillows and shriek out rage against our parents, or deep-breathe to the point of hyperventilation to re-experience past traumas, perhaps even reliving our birth to recover from the shock of leaving the womb.

According to the aforementioned personal-growth gurus, after we undergo a cathartic experience in therapy, we emerge reborn and renewed. Our pain now released, we experience wholeness and unity within ourselves. All is sweetness and light.

It all sounds great, and to be fair, some have found these experiences very helpful in their recovery process. However, dramatic cathartic experiences are not for everyone. Indeed, many of us are uncomfortable with them. Often when starting with new clients, I have to reassure them that therapy does not require them to rant and rave. To comfort them I say, "Some people think that therapy involves a lot of beating pillows and yelling and screaming. But I only do that if your check bounces." In a more serious vein, I tell them that working through old wounds often involves revisiting painful experiences and emotions, but this doesn't necessarily have to be done in a dramatic fashion. There is no one-size-fits-all solution. If they feel resistant to a certain process, there's a good chance it doesn't fit their personality and temperament. Rather than automatically accusing them of self-sabotage, it is my job to explore their resistance with them. If they conclude it's because they find the process I'm using to be embarrassing and awkward, then it's up to me to use a different process more suited to their personal style.

## Why Good Therapy Makes Bad Entertainment

Part of our belief that catharsis and drama are requirements of therapy comes from movies and TV. Most of Hollywood's portrayal of therapists and therapy ranges from inaccurate to absurd. That's because good entertainment and good therapy are two different things. For a show to be gripping, there must be conflict. Exciting things must happen in every scene or viewers get bored. Thus therapy is often portrayed as a venue where clients rage, cry, and sometimes even attack their therapists verbally or physically. And since we like definite endings, once the client has his catharsis, therapy is over and the show comes to a dramatic close. The client is now healed and ready to walk off into a glorious future.

Since love and sex are also necessary to a good plot, you often see movies where a client falls in love with his or her gorgeous, athletic therapist and they end up having passionate sex. I hate to disappoint movie buffs, but this is totally unrealistic. Most therapists are nowhere near to being gorgeous or athletic. Let's face it, we're talking about people who spend eight hours a day sitting comatose in a chair. The only exercise we get is passing a box of Kleenex to a weeping client.

And you know how runners get shin splints and knee injuries from overuse? As therapists, the only overuse injury we get is when our butt falls asleep. When I was in therapy, just the thought of sleeping with my therapist would have made me want to drastically increase my antidepressants.

But seriously, sex between a therapist and client is a huge boundary violation. And yes, it does sometimes occur in real life, but according to Hollywood it seems to happen almost as a matter of course.

Accurate portrayals of therapy also never make it onto the silver screen because good therapy is boring. When I was in therapy, long periods went by when it seemed like nothing much was happening. But that was because my therapist had fallen asleep. Now, I didn't mind her dozing off occasionally in a session, but I drew the line when she started showing up in pajamas! Be that as it may, progress in therapy can sometimes be slow and laborious, without excitement and drama. Sometimes clients go round and round, over and over the same issue, taking months or even years to reach some sort of resolution. I realize this description doesn't make therapy sound all that appealing, but working through problems that may have been there for years can take time.

If we realized how slow and boring therapy can be, we would be much less afraid of it. And we would also be quicker to resist embarrassing exercises like pillow-hugging if we knew they were not an absolute requirement of the healing process.

## What's the Difference between Shame and Embarrassment?

Jeff was having a great time, despite the fact he hardly knew anyone in the room. Everything he said evoked gales of laughter, and he loved being the life of the party. When someone mentioned Tourette's Syndrome, he just couldn't resist doing his impression of the Tourette's Family on Christmas morning. As the laughter subsided, Anita, another guest, said, "I can't laugh at that because my son has Tourette's, and it's been devastating." Silence filled the room, and it took Jeff several moments before he could respond. Unfortunately, instead of apologizing, Jeff tried to rationalize his comments with statements like, "I was just joking; it's no big deal." It seemed like Jeff was in a manure pit, and the more he tried to shovel, the deeper he sank. Soon afterwards, mired knee-deep, he fled the party, telling himself that those damned politically correct people were way too sensitive and had spoiled his fun.

Cindy thought the dress code for the meeting was supposed to be casual, but one look at all the well-dressed people told her she was sadly mistaken. She felt incredibly self-conscious in her jeans and sweatshirt. Her confidence vanished, and she thought, "This serves me right for being so stupid. I'm such an idiot and I deserve to pay for it."

Cindy and Jeff's reactions illustrate the difference between embarrassment and shame. Jeff felt embarrassed by his comments regarding Tourette's Syndrome. His feeling of embarrassment was both situation-specific and constructive. It focused on a particular behavior, and its intent was to make sure Jeff didn't repeat this mistake. Now to be fair, Jeff's impression of the Tourette's Family on Christmas morning was highly amusing, and he had no way of knowing that Anita's son had Tourette's. But whether or not Anita overreacted or whether or not Jeff's humor was in bad taste is not the issue. I leave that to the guardians of political correctness to decide. However, when we are told in front of a group we hardly know that something we have done is offensive, there is a good chance we will feel embarrassed and not want to repeat this experience again.

Conversely, Cindy's shame was global, pervading her whole being. Rather than focus on her mistake, her shame negated her value as a person. She felt like there was something wrong with her, that she was dreadfully flawed. And, unlike Jeff's embarrassment, there was nothing constructive about Cindy's shame. It just told her that she was a bad person overall and there was nothing she could do about it.

Shame is usually unhealthy because it nullifies our value as human beings rather than correcting our behavior or protecting us from emotionally damaging situations. If we experience it regularly, chances are good that we have low self-esteem caused by some wound to our soul.

According to John Bradshaw, who has written extensively on this subject, shame-based people are usually survivors of physical, sexual, or emotional abuse. These categories of abuse also include among other things, being the target of bullying or prejudice due to ethnicity, skin color, sexual orientation, disability, gender, appearance, and socioeconomic status.

Shame-based people were often abused at a young age when they lacked the intellectual capacity to understand that the abuse was not their fault. Instead, they emerged feeling they were to blame and must be very bad to warrant this kind of treatment. As adults they often feel worthless, and their shame is easily triggered. The shame they feel, as exemplified by Cindy, is almost always disproportionate to the situation or behavior that triggered it. Unlike embarrassment, shame is something we should work to lessen. A combination of therapy, support groups, workshops, and self-help books can help.

In my opinion, shame is only warranted if we do something truly shameful, like betraying a friend or cheating on a spouse. Then again, if we play our cards right, these transgressions can get us our own reality TV show. But in a serious vein, I think the people who created and ran the concentration camps in World War II should feel shame, likewise the people who carried out the genocide in Rwanda, the ethnic cleansing in the Balkans, or anyone who commits crimes against humanity. I realize that everyone has their own definition of what they consider shameful, and it's not my desire act as a moral authority. I merely use these examples to make the point that sometimes shame is, or should be, a proportionate reaction to something we've done. And in some cases, nothing less than crippling shame stands a chance of sufficiently motivating perpetrators to attempt amends and truly change who they are. And in many cases even shame is not enough.

## The Happy Neurotic Way to Cope with Shame and Embarrassment

Unfortunately, we confuse shame and embarrassment. As Happy Neurotics our goal is to channel our negative emotions in ways that build self-worth. To do this we must know which emotion we are working with, for both shame and embarrassment give us important messages, and the strategies for dealing with each are different.

To recap, embarrassment is situation specific and constructive. We might feel embarrassed because we told a tasteless joke to coworkers, or because we actually paid to go to a workshop where we had to hug total strangers, sharing with them our deep emotional pain. We might also feel embarrassed because we inappropriately dominated a conversation or made an insensitive remark. As Happy Neurotics we use our embarrassment as motivation to make amends for inappropriate behavior, to protect ourselves in situations that render us vulnerable and exposed, and to learn some life lessons. Once we've made amends or set boundaries, we come away feeling somewhat better, which is what building self-esteem is all about. We can tell ourselves that even though we blew it, we did the right thing by offering an apology and learning from our mistake. Or we experience the personal satisfaction that comes from learning how and when to stand up for ourselves in a healthy manner.

Conversely, if we rationalize or push away our embarrassment, as Jeff did, we end up feeling like jerks. Our self-esteem is undermined because no matter how much we try and deny it, we know we did something wrong, or something that hurt someone, and didn't do anything to correct or learn from it. If we do this regularly, we begin to feel the shame that arises from knowing we have a problem that we're not willing to address. By continually pushing away our embarrassment we can go from "I really blew it in that situation" to "I don't like who I am." We also run the risk of turning into jerks who attempt to defuse our own shame by shaming and blaming others for our mistakes. Ignoring our embarrassment or anger when we are the targets of inappropriate comments or requests also damages our self-esteem. We feel ashamed that we didn't say or do something to protect ourselves, and the shame increases if we allow these boundary violations to occur regularly.

Shame is an overall feeling of "I'm a bad person," and is a signal that something inside needs healing. Because the wound is often at a deep level, working with shame and channeling it in ways that build self-esteem can be a long process. To begin with, just being able to identify it is a huge step. My clients often feel great relief upon realizing this horrible, debilitating feeling they experience on a regular basis has a name. And the act of reaching out for help also builds a positive self-image, because it feels good to finally be taking care of a problem that has existed for so long.

The next step is to understand the causes of our shame. This frequently requires going to therapy, attending workshops, and learning to use emotional logic, as in seeing where we disproportionately react with shame. Realizing that our shame makes sense, and that whatever caused it was not our fault also helps us feel better about ourselves. Further steps towards healing occur when we grieve the abuse we suffered and talk about our feelings with people who love and support us. Every step we take towards recovery helps us feel more positive towards ourselves.

As Happy Neurotics, we know our recovery will never be perfect or absolute. We also know it will never be a straight line. Carl Jung described it best when he said therapy is more of a spiral process, where we go past the same issues again and again but each time on a deeper level that is closer to the core. Or you can look at it in a more holistic way: As our issues decrease, so does our bank balance. Whether or not we have any money left, in time our shame lessens, but some demons may still remain, rearing their ugly heads when we least expect it. At these times, we cope by applying our Happy Neurotic repertoire of tools and knowledge.

## Three Key Questions for Dealing with Embarrassment

Embarrassment is situation-specific and happens in real time, versus the tendency of shame to warp time and make us feel like we are five years old again. Thus, the strategies for dealing with embarrassment are much more short-term and focused on the present. By using the Three Key Questions for Dealing with Embarrassment, we can learn to manage it in a healthier fashion. We can ask ourselves these questions:

1. "What is it about this situation that I find embarrassing?"

2. "Is there something I need to do or say to defuse my embarrassment?"
3. "Is there something I need to accept?"

By asking these questions, we pinpoint the source of our embarrassment, then decide on appropriate means of addressing and/or coping with it. Even if we can't isolate the exact cause, we can still decide whether we need to take some sort of action and/or accept that we are embarrassed and move on with things.

Had I asked myself the Three Key Questions for Dealing with Embarrassment at the seminar where we had to hold hands with strangers and look deeply into their eyes, it would have gone like this:

1. "What is it about this situation that I find embarrassing?"
*"I find it embarrassing to have to look a stranger in the eye and hold his hands."*
2. "Is there something I need to do or say to defuse my embarrassment?"
*"I need to pass on this exercise."*
3. "Is there something I need to accept?"
*"I need to accept that it's okay for me to feel embarrassed, and take appropriate steps to protect myself. I also may need to accept that this seminar is not for me."*

Had Jeff asked himself the Three Key Questions for Dealing with Embarrassment when he made those insensitive jokes about Tourette's Syndrome, it might have gone like this:
1. "What is it about this situation that I find embarrassing?"
*"I'm really embarrassed that I've inadvertently offended someone with my jokes about Tourette's Syndrome."*
2. "Is there something I need to do or say to defuse my embarrassment?"
*"I need to apologize to her."*
3. "Is there something I need to accept?"
*"I need to accept that not everyone shares my sense of humor, and that if I make jokes about things like Tourette's Syndrome, some people may be offended. I also need to accept that I should probably be more careful about where I make these kinds of jokes."*

## How to Make Amends when You've Put Your Foot in Your Mouth

Sometimes, the problem with making amends when we've behaved inappropriately is not that we don't want to but that we don't know how. We offer an awkward apology, then negate it by attempting to rationalize or explain away our behavior. "Sorry I made that joke, but my other friends think it's really funny, and besides, I've had a long day, I'm tired, and it just sort of slipped out." On top of negating our apology, we also indirectly ask the person we've wronged for sympathy and understanding. Is it any wonder the situation never gets resolved?

To effectively make amends, we must do four things:

1. Clearly and directly apologize, without rationalizing or explaining away our behavior. "I'm sorry I made that joke; I can see it really hurt you."
2. Give the other person a chance to communicate how our behavior affected her. "How are you doing with all this?"
3. Communicate empathy, our understanding of how our behavior affected the other person, by paraphrasing what they say in our own words. "So you were really hurt by my comments."
This step is especially important, because when people feel we understand them, it lessens their hurt and anger.
4. State what we've learned from the situation and our intent to change. "I've learned that some things that are funny to me aren't funny to others and that in future I need to be aware of that."

Is this a perfect solution that will immediately fix everything to do with feeling embarrassment? Will this enable you to take a quantum leap in your personal growth? No. As Happy Neurotics we know better than to expect that. But we can certainly come away from a situation where we blew it, telling ourselves we took responsibility and did everything possible to remedy things.

## How to Stand Up for Yourself, Whether They Like It or Not

To this day I regret not setting a boundary at the seminar where they got me to say, "I love you" to a pillow. I felt stupid doing it and stupid for not standing up for myself. We all have the right to draw the line when we feel uncomfortable with something.

The problem is, when stating our limits we sometimes feel obligated to get the other person's approval by explaining why, and end up negating ourselves: "I'm sorry. I'm just not comfortable with this exercise. I guess maybe I'm blocked, or I haven't done enough work on myself. Is it okay if I pass on this one?" Instead of assertively stating our limits, we weasel out of doing something by portraying ourselves as deficient and inadequate. Then we come away feeling embarrassed that in setting limits we undermined ourselves.

Newsflash: We don't need someone else's approval to set boundaries. We don't need to explain our reasons or ask for permission. Setting boundaries is something we have a right to do unilaterally. All we need to say is, "I'm really uncomfortable with this, so I'm going to pass," or "I found that comment embarrassing; I'd appreciate it if you don't say something like that again."

As Happy Neurotics, our task is to use embarrassment and shame in ways that build our self-esteem. Being able to set appropriate boundaries helps us to do that. But before we get ahead of ourselves, let's do a Happy Neurotic reality check.

Now that we've read this section, will boundary-setting phrases easily and quickly trip off our tongues? Will this information dramatically change our lives, giving us total control and confidence in any situation? Nope. Boundary setting is a difficult skill that takes time and effort to develop. I have yet to meet anyone for whom it feels totally comfortable. I can guarantee you will make mistakes, perhaps falling back into apologizing for yourself, or setting boundaries too quickly by using a sledgehammer instead of a stop sign. You may rarely come away thinking, "I did it just right," but you probably will come away thinking. "I did it better than last time," or "I did it well enough," or "Even though there's lots of room for improvement, at least I stood up for myself." And it's in the doing it "well enough," or the doing it "better than last time," or the "at least I stood up for myself" that our self-esteem grows.

# I'M ONE WITH THE UNIVERSE, SO WHY DO I HAVE ALL THESE NAGGING DOUBTS?

## Why Happy Neurotics Should Give Their Inner Skeptic a Front Row Seat

"Clasp your hands together with the palms open and facing each other."

We put our hands in the prayer pose as the speaker directed. Then there was a moment of silence.

"Now take your hands and rub them together like you were washing them."

Again the group did as she said.

"A minute ago, who here felt uncomfortable because they thought I was going to make you pray?"

Several people including myself raised their hands.

"This exercise shows how you approach new experiences. If you thought I was going to make you pray, it means that you approach situations and people with suspicion. And remember, if you do that, you will create a negative reality. But if you just stayed open to the possibilities and didn't feel the need to protect yourself, it means you approach the universe with trust, and that trust will attract good energy towards you."

Quite frankly, I just felt like I'd been manipulated. First of all, I'd only met the speaker two minutes previously, so why should I trust her? Trust is earned over time. And in terms of trusting the situation,

119

I'd been to seminars where speakers *had* asked their audience to pray, so it's not like my suspicion was totally unjustified.

The truth was, I and the others had been set up. The speaker had created an experience that had negative associations for many people, and then told us we were wrong for having negative associations.

She was telling us not to trust our feelings, when the wise thing to do when something reminds you of or symbolizes a bad or questionable experience, is to proceed with caution, not dive in headfirst. If a stranger calls and says you've won a big prize, but first you have to give him $5,000 in cash as a deposit, the smart thing to do is be very, very skeptical. And in the highly unlikely possibility this offer is legitimate, your skeptical reaction is still a healthy response to being asked to give $5,000 to a stranger. Furthermore, if you have been swindled at some point in your life, chances are you will be extra skeptical the next time someone approaches you with anything resembling a con.

## Why We Don't Like Skeptics

The dictionary defines skepticism as a "doubting, questioning, or suspicious attitude, disposition or state of mind." Not a very fashionable quality in our "trust the universe" culture of personal development. And we know it. New Agey people often proudly say, "I just trust that things will work out; the universe always provides." But you seldom hear them boastfully declare, "I'm a suspicious, doubting kind of person. The universe scares the heck out of me." And which of these attitudes makes the most sense? Let me put it this way: Along with all the beauty of nature, the universe also created disease, natural disasters, and politicians, all of which should terrify any thinking person.

And let me digress for a moment. The "trust the universers" spout off about living in harmony with nature. Have these folks taken a good look at what happens in nature? Everywhere you turn, creatures are ruthlessly killing and feeding on each other. I can just imagine living that way. Each day I'd get up and figure out which neighbor I'd stalk and eat for dinner. And there'd be some fringe benefits too. Once I did away with him, I'd also get his parking spot. That would be one way to solve the overcrowding on my block! And living nature's way would also change the way I parent. Instead of teaching my kid to ride a bike, I'd teach him to skin and bone his grade one teacher.

Personally, I'm glad we humans don't live in harmony with nature, spending all our time looking for prey to kill. Thanks to our large brains we have evolved into more civilized pursuits like going to monster truck pulls and downloading Internet porn.

But back to this skepticism thing. Unfortunately, the words "doubt" and "suspicion" evoke negative associations. In our culture of positivity, people with these qualities are seen as killjoys. "There she goes again—asking more of those questions. Why can't she just trust things will work out?" They are accused of "doing it wrong," "not getting it," or being "too negative." Sometimes they are even ostracized for refusing to uncritically accept the teachings handed down by the seminar leader.

Skeptics make us uncomfortable. They make us look at things we'd rather not. They question when we're told we can achieve real happiness and total confidence in just 21 days or our money back. In a personal development milieu that values striving for inner peace and harmony, this is the wrong thing to do.

I attended an introductory evening for a seminar on universal wisdom given by a woman claiming to be a "walk-in," an extraterrestrial in a human body. Since she claimed the ability to communicate telepathically and astral travel, I wanted to know why she had to advertise her seminar in a local New Age magazine and take a bus to the workshop venue.

But all kidding aside, I did attend a seminar on universal wisdom given by a walk-in. Since she claimed the ability to communicate telepathically and astral travel, I wanted to know why she had to advertise her seminar in a local New Age magazine and take a bus to the workshop venue. I also wanted to see her demonstrate these amazing powers. I figure if someone bases her credibility on a certain claim, it's reasonable to ask her to back it up. If someone asks me to invest in a mutual fund, maintaining I will double my money in a year, it's legitimate to ask for proof that the fund is such a hot commodity. Should my skepticism be met with condescension or equivocation, I'd be a fool to move forward.

My skepticism at the extraterrestrial evening was met with just that. As far as the faithful were concerned, I had "trust issues" and was not at a point in my spiritual development where I could be expected to grasp such exalted teachings. I wish I had responded, "In that case, you're not at a point in your financial development where you get to grasp my check." And yes, that would've been a childish response I may have later regretted, but as a Happy Neurotic I'm allowed to occasionally screw up.

We frequently want to believe seminar leaders when they say we can quickly, easily attain unlimited wealth and abundance, achieve perfect health, and reverse the aging process. Often paying big bucks to attend their programs, we can have a strong stake in maintaining these beliefs so we don't feel like we've wasted our money. But those nagging doubts are hard to avoid when a skeptic asks what the $3,000 seminar on "How to Make a Million Dollars by Eliminating Negative Thinking" did for us. Instead of expressing doubt, we may sidestep, replying with something like, "Well, it takes a long time; I've still got a lot of work to do. You can't expect results right away [even though that's what the seminar ads promised], and besides, you don't understand—it's way more complicated than that."

## Embrace Your Inner Skeptic

Two forces have battled since the beginning of time: The desire to believe, and the need to protect ourselves. When these two components, openness and skepticism, are well balanced, we usually make good choices. Think of it this way: On one hand there is our child-like part that wants to believe almost anything or anyone that tells him what he wants to hear. Then there's our adult inner skeptic, which likes to see some sort of proof. As Happy Neurotics we need both the trusting child and the adult skeptic. We want to remain open and not lose our sense of wonder, for without it, we become overly cynical and bitter. However, it's a dangerous world out there, and we need to protect ourselves from making bad choices.

The problem occurs when child and skeptic become disconnected. Throughout the ages, people have believed in all sorts of outrageous things, like miracle cures, get rich quick schemes, and false messiahs, even when there was no evidence to support any of their claims. There was a televangelist whose "direct channel to God" gave him amazing knowledge of audience members' private issues. It turned out that his direct channel to God was an elaborate ruse involving information fed to him by his wife via a hidden microphone and earpiece. (I wonder if, in addition to sending him audience information, his wife ever took the opportunity via the hidden microphone to remind our tele-vangelist to take out the garbage or put the toilet seat down?)

His hoax was exposed on national TV, yet some continued to believe and generously finance his cause. They had stopped listening to their adult skeptic and were being run by their child. Anyone who has been a parent knows that children need to have input, but it's up to the adult to make the final decision. If not guided by us, children will make all sorts of unwise and potentially dangerous decisions.

Allowing the child to run us and uncritically accept questionable philosophies and belief systems also damages our self-esteem. We look back at some of the things we did or said and feel foolish, thinking, "I can't believe I said 'I love you' to a pillow. How embarrassing. I wish I'd said 'No, I won't do that.'" In chapter seven you learned that embarrassment tells us to set boundaries and protect ourselves. It is often our skepticism that gives us the energy necessary to set the boundaries in the first place. It is as though the adult all of a sudden appears and says, "Hey, wait a second, what's going on here? Why are we doing this?"

## Skepticism: The Route to Personal Empowerment

Skepticism protects and empowers us. We may desperately want to believe that if we think only positive thoughts, nothing bad will ever happen to us. But on some level we remain skeptical. That skeptical part of us naturally wants to ask questions like, "What evidence is this belief based on?"

It also motivates us to look around and see if this belief fits with our experience of life. When we accept or reject a belief based on our own analysis, we feel empowered. We also feel a sense of ownership because the belief is now truly ours. But by unquestioningly believing, we abdicate the ability to think and make choices for ourselves, forego-ing these important building blocks of a positive self-image. Instead, we become like children, automatically parroting what the teacher says. All we learn is to depend on others to give us the answer, not figure it out ourselves. German playwright Johann von Goethe said: "All truly wise thoughts have been thought already thousands of times, but to make them truly ours we must think them over again honestly until they take root in our personal experience."

## It's Not What You Believe but How You Get There

What we choose to believe is less important than the process we use to arrive at our chosen belief. I know people who have had very powerful experiences during past life regressions. Though previously skeptical, they now believe in reincarnation because it accords with their personal life experience. I also know people who don't believe in past lives because they lack scientific proof or a meaningful experience of them. Both groups arrived at their beliefs not through a process of blind faith, but through a process of working through their skepticism. Thus both groups' beliefs, though at odds with each other, are meaningful and empowering for each individual believer.

On the other hand, there are the flavor-of-the-month-club believers. One month it's past lives, the next it's alien abductions, the power of positive thinking, crystal healing, Course in Miracles, and on and on. What these believers have in common is a need to believe in something, and the desire for a quick fix, which they allow to drown out their skepticism. Since their beliefs are not arrived at through personal analysis and experience, they have no sense of ownership, and thus constantly change belief systems. Their behav-ior is similar to children constantly tiring of the old toys and seek-ing new ones. Once again, the issue is not whether you believe in alien abductions, the power of positive thinking, crystal healing, and Course in Miracles; the issue is whether you got to your beliefs as an adult or as a child.

## Does the Marketing for Personal Development Products Speak to the Adult or the Child?

Anyone in sales and marketing knows that buying is based on immature emotion, not reason. Therefore the key to making a sale is to find our "hot buttons," or what therapists call our insecurities and unmet needs, and push them repeatedly. In other words, advertisers try to get us to do what they want by making us feel bad about ourselves. Personally, I don't need commercials to tell me I'm doing it wrong. That's why I have kids! But commercials can really undermine our self-image. Can you imagine if you had someone who constantly told you that you're not good enough, have bad hygiene, and look like a dork? Then again, that's the kind of person a lot of people marry.

Furthermore, companies do not sell products; they sell brands by establishing emotional ties between their brand and ourselves. Starbucks does not sell coffee; it sells the coffee experience of comfort and community. Nike does not sell runners; it sells fitness and success. These marketing campaigns speak to our child who thinks, "I gotta have that now!" The last thing advertisers want to do is activate our adult skeptic by selling us a product we can compare to other products. Our adult skeptic would say, "Why should I buy Starbucks coffee when I can get the same thing for less somewhere else?" Or it would think, "What's so great about Nike runners? Am I really getting an amazing product, or am I paying for a marketing campaign?

Similarly, the personal development industry often markets to our child. "Unlimited success can be yours . . . Learn to think like a millionaire in just two weeks . . . Conquer your fears quickly and easily . . . Look younger and reverse the aging process," are all slogans aimed at our child, who gets incredibly excited and demands that we sign up. And just like Starbucks and Nike, the last thing these marketers want to do is engage our adult skeptic, because she'll ask questions like: "How many graduates of your course are now millionaires?" "Show me proof that saying affirmations will create unlimited success in my life." "Why should I pay you $500 to tell me what affirmations to say when I can go to the library and borrow a book of affirmations for free?" "Why do you charge so much for your seminar, especially since your minions deliver it and you don't show up yourself?"

Another marketing tactic personal development gurus use to hook our child is taking something well known and pitching it like it's an amazing new discovery. All of a sudden going for a brisk walk is called "power walking," and becomes an astounding new cure for everything under the sun. Taking an afternoon nap becomes "power napping," and to do it right we must attend seminars and buy books and DVDs. Of course, our child wants to be first on the block to acquire all these incredibly cool new toys.

By the way, I'm currently developing a seminar on "power multi-tasking," where you surf channels on four TVs simultaneously while stuffing your face with Twinkies. Not only will you need to buy the workbook and DVDs from me, but also the Twinkies and the TVs. After all, you want to do it right, don't you?

If a seminar leader is willing to take the time to explain things so we can logically or experientially understand what she teaches and why it works, chances are good we're on the right track. However, if she keeps talking to our child by saying things like, "You need to trust; there are no accidents. You were guided to take this workshop. This is a once in a lifetime opportunity. If you don't hurry, the workshop will fill up," then we may want to take our business and questions elsewhere.

It also helps to understand the difference between how we feel when someone tries to engage our adult and when she tries to hook our child. When a seminar leader's words click on an adult level, we experience a sense of clarity or revelation. All of a sudden things make sense; the road ahead seems clearer and we think, "Now I get it." However, when she tries to hook our child, we feel a sense of desire and urgency—"I have to have that now. If I don't sign up immediately, it'll be too late." To which our skeptic would respond, "Do you really need this so badly, and why are you in such a hurry?"

## But What If Something Just Feels Right?

Just because we choose to be skeptical doesn't mean we can't make a decision that *feels* right. Happy Neurotics understand the difference between rational choice and empowered choice. Rational choice is entirely fact-based. We gather concrete evidence and base our decision on it. On paper, our decision may look right, but we may feel little enthusiasm, the lack of which makes it hard to move ahead and implement an action plan.

Empowered choice is stronger because it also factors in our feelings as to whether a belief system, technique, or seminar leader's personality is right for us. If someone speaks, and we feel the words strike a chord within, chances are what she said makes rational sense and accords with our life experience and intuition. It feels right *and* it fits with our experience of the world. This convergence of emotional resonance and life experience is one of the strongest forms of truth. Any choice we make based on it is bound to feel empowering.

The world of spirituality is a world of subjectivity. Until now, science has been unable to conclusively prove the existence of things like spirits and past lives. In the spiritual realm, we tend to believe what clicks with us and fits with our personal experience, science be damned. And in the world of personal development and therapy, subjectivity is also a key element. The effectiveness of a seminar or therapeutic technique hinges on how well it and the personality of the speaker or counselor click with us. What creates a transformational experience for some does nothing for others. For both spirituality and personal development, we often arrive at our beliefs first, then come across information confirming what we already know.

## The Three Key Questions for Dealing with Skepticism

As Happy Neurotics, we understand that skepticism is another one of those negative emotions we need to channel in positive ways that build self-esteem. Rather than attacking a seminar leader or proponent of a certain belief system, we use our skepticism to make an empowered choice by instead asking three questions, two of which are subjective, and one which is objective:

1. "Does this feel right to me? Is there some sort of inner click or resonance?"

2. "Does this fit with my experience of life?"
3. "What evidence is there to support what this person says?"

John Bradshaw's books on dysfunctional families were a huge hit because many readers could answer "Yes" to all three of these questions when they considered his ideas. What he said resonated with them, they could see it play out in their own lives, *and* it was backed by research.

Conversely, let's get back to the saying of "I love you" to a pillow. Had I asked, "Does this feel right to me?" my answer would have been a resounding "No." Had I then asked, "Does the belief that I will be healed by saying "I love you" to a pillow fit with my experience of life?" I would have also answered "No." In terms of empirical evidence to support that saying "I love you" to a pillow would heal me, all I had was the leader's opinion. In this case, there was a convergence between emotional resonance and personal experience, which had I listened to, would have empowered me to say "No" to the exercise.

## Don't Mistake Infatuation for the Real Thing

When first encountering a new personal development or spiritual teaching, we often go through a period of infatuation, similar to the infatuation at the beginning of a relationship. Just as with a new love, the new teaching takes on a larger-than-life quality. We idealize it and the person teaching it. We think we've finally found the answer to all our problems, and from here on, everything will be radically different. This effect is intensified if we've just been to a powerful workshop and gotten swept away by the group's energy. The child firmly at the wheel, our skeptic is now relegated to the back seat.

During the infatuation period of a relationship we want to tell everyone about our new love and how amazing he or she is. The same goes for the new teaching. It can take on religious overtones as we go out and proselytize to the world about our newly discovered faith. Maybe you've bumped into someone like this who insists on trying to sign you up for a workshop he's just taken. Not only won't he take "no" for an answer; he is determined to share his newly acquired wisdom every time you meet. He wants you to have a life just like his, even if you're not interested. Most annoying of all, he insists on inculcating you with all the jargon that he's learned from his new master. Everything is a "transformational experience," "an opportunity to become one with spirit," "a chance to let go of your poverty consciousness," and "a sure-fire path to unlimited abundance that is your birthright as a being of love and light."

These people are called "assholes." You must avoid them at all costs. Don't feel bad if you have to make any excuse you can think of to avoid "sharing" with them. After a while, most of them lose their zealotry and are capable of carrying on regular conversations. I myself have been an asshole more than once, and still cringe at the thought of how annoying I must have been to those around me.

As the infatuation wears off in a relationship, we begin to see the not-so-wonderful aspects of our beloved. Things that initially attracted us to her become annoying. We realize she may not be our soulmate after all. Or we spend the next few years trying to get the relationship back to where it used to be by doing the things we did in those first few glorious months of infatuation, often with little or no success.

The same can happen with our new guru and her philosophy of life. We start to see the flaws and to question her personal integrity. The principles of her program no longer seem as magical. We also yearn to get back into the space we were at when first attending her workshop. When we can't do it on our own, we frantically send away for more books and DVDs, or sign up for another workshop. Maybe we temporarily recapture that initial high, but it never seems to last.

In a relationship, if we decide that our new partner is not right for us, we often look back at the initial infatuation and feel some embarrassment. We think, "The signs were all there. How could I have missed them?" Similarly, once we fall out of love with our self-help guru, we question how we could have fallen for her program, perhaps sometimes to the point of donating numerous of hours of unpaid labor to help her further her business ends.

This is not to say we don't learn anything of value. Once free of the infatuation, we are able to see what helped us and leave the rest. We also learn that infatuation with something new is normal and to be enjoyed, but that next time we're on that journey, we need to allow our skeptic to do at least some of the driving

## What's the Difference between a Skeptic and a Pain in the Ass?

By now, everyone in the workshop on spiritual healing including myself was feeling uncomfortable. Every time the speaker attempted to convey a new idea, the man in the gray sweatshirt would argue with her. And no matter how patiently she tried to explain, he was never satisfied, and his questions increasingly took on a belligerent tone.

The man in the gray sweatshirt was, to put it bluntly, behaving like a pain in the ass. He seemed to take pleasure in being oppositional just for the sake of being oppositional. He disagreed with everything. And it also appeared he wanted to attack the speaker, to make her look stupid and ineffectual.

If you've been to workshops or seminars, you may have met this person. Or maybe you have one at work, among your friends, or even, heaven forbid, in your family. A pain in the ass is basically a jerk, someone who expresses his negative emotions in ways that are hurtful to himself and others. A pain in the ass expresses his skepticism destructively, using it to wound others and inappropriately dominate conversations. A pain in the ass also has the amazing knack of being able to turn almost any discussion into a power struggle and to ruin a group experience for everyone involved. You might be thinking that no one can ruin something for you unless you let them. But as Happy Neurotics, we know that it is perfectly healthy and normal to feel frustrated, disappointed, or angry when someone attacks a speaker and makes it impossible for us to get much out of his or her presentation.

As you've just learned, the purpose of healthy skepticism is to empower us and give us ownership over our beliefs. A Happy Neurotic knows that feeling skeptical is a sign that she needs to ask the Three Key Questions for Dealing with Skepticism. Her attitude is one of curiosity, seeking answers to legitimate questions in ways that don't ruin things for others.

There is nothing empowering about being a pain in the ass, because the outcome of this behavior is predetermined, almost always leading to a rejection of other people and their ideas. The pain in the ass rejects because he has a strong need to reject, just as the flavor-of-the-month-club believer believes because she has a strong need to believe. Neither of these behaviors allows them to develop a healthy self-image by thinking and choosing for themselves. Instead, they are controlled by their strong need to reject or accept.

## How To Be Skeptical and Get Information without Creating a Power Struggle

A counseling instructor of mine once commented that Peter Falk on the TV show *Columbo* was his role model. Peter Falk played Lieutenant Columbo, a bumbling detective who had an uncanny knack of solving homicides. Columbo's modus operandi was to get to know the suspect in a non-threatening way. Rather than accusing and finger-pointing, he would ask the suspect's help in understanding various facets of the crime. By making someone else the expert he avoided a power struggle as he elicited the information needed to make his case. People like to be asked their opinion, since for most of us, what we think is the most fascinating thing in the world. Columbo's questions usually began with, "Could you help me to understand . . . ?" or, "What do you think about . . . ?" Sooner or later the suspect would divulge incriminating information and Columbo would have his conviction.

Though we're not detectives solving homicides, I think Columbo's principles are sound for us too. When we are skeptical, by allowing the other person to be the expert and explain things to us, we get the information we need without creating a power struggle or evoking defensive reactions. And once we have what we need, we can politely and firmly make a decision that is right for us from an adult perspective. The difference between the man in the gray sweatshirt's style and our non-confrontational approach is that we are not trying to get someone to incriminate himself, or make him look stupid. In our version of Columbo, the goal is to let other person have his beliefs, while at the same time using our skepticism to elicit information and determine where we stand.

## WHAT IF MY FEARS WON'T GO AWAY?

### It's a Scary World—No Wonder You're Still Afraid

In this book, you've learned that fear and self-doubt can be productive as long as you know what to do with these feelings. But here's where it gets confusing: If you *are* able to figure out exactly what you fear and take action, you create success and build self-esteem. But in the world of feelings, things are often not that clear. Many of us have existential fears and doubts rattling around in our heads. These fears are usually about things we can't control, like getting cancer, someone abducting our children, our spouse dying of a heart attack, or the stock market crashing.

At its essence, existential fear isn't really about the events it attaches itself to. It's about fear of death and tragedy. The truth is, that for all our advanced technology, we are still small, vulnerable creatures living in a big, scary world, and nothing can change that.

This fact is constantly brought home to us by the media, which inundates us with stories of disaster, violence, and death. And here's the crazy-making thing: On the one hand, horrific events are brought into our homes through the media on a daily basis, creating fear that is for many of us disproportionate to our everyday reality. On the other hand, these things *could* happen, so part of our fear is based in reality.

Let's say you're afraid of a home invasion because you keep hearing about them in the news. Yet you live in a safe neighborhood where the

133

chances of this happening are equal to your chances of winning the lottery. Do you still take actions like buying a gun or putting bars on all your windows and doors? And what about food poisoning? There's a remote chance that could happen to you. Do you rigorously research every store and restaurant you patronize by calling the health department and asking for a report? And what if they missed something? There may be a one-in-a-million chance they did, so do you conduct your own inspection of each place? And what if, on the way to conduct your inspection, you are struck by lightning? It *does* happen, so maybe you should wear a rubber suit so you don't get fried. How do you take action on all these things without having a nervous breakdown?

## A New Way of Understanding Fear

The answer is that, in general, you don't. Here's an example: A client named Albert reported feeling anxiety. When I asked him to specify, he said that he feared a home invasion by a gang of psychopathic drug users. When I asked, "If you had unlimited resources, what would you do to protect yourself?" Albert said he'd build a huge wall around his house, hire armed guards, and have firearms in every room. Then I asked if these measures would make him feel safe. "No," he replied, because then he would worry about someone poisoning his food, bribing the guards to turn against him, or somehow penetrating his security system. And if I could magically guarantee that those things wouldn't happen, I asked him, then would he feel completely safe? No, because then he'd worry about global warming, nuclear war, or some other human-made disaster that would eliminate our species. And if we could rule out human-made disasters, then he'd worry about a meteor hitting the earth and wiping out life as we know it. The point is that no matter what safeguards I suggested, Albert was still afraid.

Albert did not have a mental illness. He also lived in a safe neighborhood, had never been assaulted, and had no involvement with drug dealers or other criminal elements. He did not seriously contemplate turning his house into an impregnable fortress. His fortress fantasy was a symbol of his fear and powerlessness. Seeking counseling to eliminate his anxiety, he was less than thrilled to hear me state,

"Some of the fear you have makes total sense, and there's no action you can take to make all your fear go away."

Albert soon learned what all Happy Neurotics come to realize: Because we are small, vulnerable beings in a big, scary world where terrible things happen, it's normal to have a certain amount of existential fear. The challenge is to shift the way we understand it. In the old model (and the New Age one), fear is a bad thing and must be eliminated. Even during World War II, Franklin Roosevelt said: "The only thing we have to fear is fear itself." I humbly disagree. Fear is not the enemy. The enemy is a *lack* of fear. If people were more afraid, they wouldn't go to war in the first place. Can you imagine if all the members of every army, terrorist group, or militia in the world were so afraid that they refused to show up for any hostilities whatsoever? We'd have to find an alternative to war where no one got hurt! As a matter of fact, a study conducted in Montreal found that boys in neighborhoods with high crime rates who avoided getting into trouble have higher levels of the stress hormone cortisol than their more violent peers. The researchers concluded that having high stress levels made these boys more afraid and less likely to partake in risky activities like committing crimes or getting into fights. It seems that in these neighborhoods, it's the scaredy cats, not the tough guys, who tend to survive.

In the new model presented in this book, fear is in fact a good thing—if you understand it properly. The challenge is not getting all of it to disappear, because chances are you won't, no matter how much personal growth work you do. During a powerful seminar experience it may lift for a while, and in the course of everyday life it may wax and wane, but some of our fear will probably always return in some form. In the new model, the challenge is to understand the difference between existential fears, which for most of us are a fact of life, and specific fears that we can reduce or get rid of by taking action.

## What If I Have So Many Fears that I Can't Tell Them Apart?

As previously stated, existential fear is really fear of death and tragedy, which attaches itself to events like getting a terminal illness, dying in a fire, or being the victim of a home invasion. But sometimes it's hard to tell the difference between existential fear attaching itself to some unlikely hypothetical situation, and a specific fear that we need to take action on. The Existential and Specific Fear Assessment helped Albert and can also help you to tell the difference.

### Existential and Specific Fear Assessment

**Step One:** You catch yourself worrying.

Ask, "What am I worried about or afraid of?"

**Step Two:** Ask, "Do I have a good reason to believe that this fear could likely come to pass?"

If yes, what concrete things lead me to believe that?

If no, what concrete things lead me to believe that?

Please note: concrete things are not stories you've heard in the news about things that happened to someone else. They are conditions present in your life that could justify your fears. For example, if you fear being robbed and you live in or frequent a dangerous neighborhood, then you have concrete conditions to base your fear on. But at this point in the assessment, if you have no concrete reasons to believe your fear will come to pass, then you can identify it as existential. If you do have reasons to believe your fear might happen, continue to Step Three.

**Step Three:** Ask, "Is there any action I need to take?"

If yes, what and when? Will taking this action significantly reduce or eliminate this fear?

If yes, then your fear is specific. If you still feel anxious, go to Step Four.

**Step Four:** Ask, "Could something else be causing my anxiety? If so, what?"

If yes, once you've figured out what it is, then go back to Step Two.

If you notice that every time you get to Step Four you come up with a new fear, then, as in Albert's case, the issue probably isn't specific fear,but existential fear attaching itself to certain events.

Now let's take an actual fear through the steps of the Existential and Specific Fear Assessment. The reason we do these steps is to concretize the fear and get a really good look at it. Once we do, it can lose its power, even become absurd. I'll never forget the scene in *The Wizard of Oz* where Dorothy finally comes face to face with the wizard. Viewed from the front, he is this huge head with a booming voice, but when she walks behind the head she finds it being run by this scared little guy. Similarly, viewed head-on, some of the things we fear can seem huge, but on further investigation they may lose some of their menace.

That being said, the goal of the Existential and Specific Fear Assessment isn't to make the fear go away (though sometimes this is the result); it's to help separate our fears into things that we need to take action on, and things we need to accept and cope with.

### Existential and Specific Fear Assessment #2

**Step One:** All of a sudden, you catch yourself worrying.

Ask, "What am I worried about or afraid of?"

*I'm worried that my house will burn down.*

**Step Two:** Ask, "Do I have a good reason to believe that this fear could likely come to pass?"

*No, I don't have a good reason to believe this will happen.*

If no, what concrete things lead me to believe that?

*Our house is well maintained and we have no fire hazards.*

Due to a lack of concrete specifics, it's obvious that my fear is existential. I can stop now and go to the next section in this chapter on how to deal with existential fear (Fear of Death: The Key to Appreciating Life).

Let's take another example:

### Existential and Specific Fear Assessment #3

**Step One:** All of a sudden, you catch yourself worrying.

Ask, "What am I worried about or afraid of?"

*I'm worried that my house will burn down.*

**Step Two:** Ask, "Do I have a good reason to believe that this fear could likely come to pass?"

*Yes.*

If yes, what concrete things lead me to believe that?

*Our basement is a mess, it's full of old newspapers, there is a propane tank near the heater along with several large containers of paint thinner, and my kids love to play with matches.*

At this point it's obvious that my fear is specific, so I continue to Step Three.

**Step Three:** Ask, "Is there any action I need to take?"

If yes, what and when?

*I need to clean up the basement, get rid of all the flammable material tomorrow, and buy the kids some new video games to get their minds off of lighting matches.*

At this point I will take action and presumably my fear will be eliminated or significantly reduced. But if I take action and my fear still remains, I need to go to Step Four.

**Step Four:** Ask, "Could something else be causing my anxiety?"

*Yes.*

If so, what?

*I'm worried that I could get cancer.*

Now I go back to Step Two.

**Step Two:** Ask, "Do I have a good reason to believe that this fear could likely come to pass?"

*No.*

If no, what concrete things lead me to believe that?

*I have a healthy diet, exercise regularly, and have no history of cancer in my family.*

Due to a lack of concrete specifics, it's obvious that my fear of cancer is existential. However, my fear of a house fire was specific, since it was justified by concrete conditions. Once I've taken action on that fear, I will also need to cope with my existential fear.

### Fear of Death: The Key to Appreciating Life

As I've said over and over, Happy Neurotics channel their negative emotions in productive ways that build self-worth. For specific fears, this involves taking some sort of action. However, existential fear is different, since there is no specific action we can take to make it disappear. To cope with it we must first understand its purpose. As I said earlier, existential fear is really fear of death and tragedy, and I can't think of better motivation to take good care of ourselves and make sure we get the most out of life. Fear of death and tragedy is the reason we look both ways before crossing the street, the reason we take care of our bodies, and the reason we try to make good decisions with our money. But even more than that, fear of death and tragedy makes us really appreciate our lives and the people in them. The problem is that we get so focused on the hypothetical events our fear attaches to, such as being robbed, getting cancer, or having a meteor strike the earth, that we miss the whole point of why the fear is there in the first place. Our job is not to make the fear go away; it's to detach from the hypothetical event our existential fear has attached itself to. Then we can use the energy from the existential fear to affirm life.

## The "Financial Planner from Hell" Technique

When clients tell me they catastrophize through dwelling on existential fears on a regular basis, I ask, "How often has your inner catastrophizer been right? How often has it accurately predicted the future?" The answer is usually "Never" or "Almost never." Then I ask: "Would you invest all your money on the advice of a financial planner who had a failure rate of almost 100 percent? Would you trust that individual for accurate market forecasts? Would you get excited if she foresaw a bull market, or freak out if she anticipated a crash? Would you recommend her services to your friends? If not, why do you put so much faith in your inner catastrophizer, given her pitiful track record?"

From then on, my clients' homework is to use the "Financial Planner from Hell" Technique to detach from whatever hypothetical events their existential fear attaches to. That means that when they start worrying about getting a terminal illness, being in a plane crash, or having their spouse suddenly drop dead, they remind themselves that their inner catastrophizer is seldom, if ever, right, and that if he was a financial planner they'd ignore everything he said—or at least take it with a large grain of salt!

## I'm Powerless and I'm Going To Die,
## But I Sure Feel Great Now!

After detaching from the events our existential fear attaches to, the next step is to deal with the underlying fear of death and tragedy. We do this by using the fear as motivation to value life. We remind ourselves that we are powerless over some things, and that sooner or later we will all die. Then we give thanks for being alive in this moment, and focus on the good things in our lives, no matter how small they are. When doing this exercise, I make it more concrete by spending a minute or two writing some of those things down on a piece of scrap paper. For me, these include the fact I have a great family, the fact I have a great wife, and the fact that she doesn't know about my three girlfriends—just kidding! Like I said earlier, Happy Neurotics have a sense of humor about all this stuff. If they don't, personal-growth work can become too serious and dogmatic, and the people doing it run the risk of becoming assholes.

Doing this exercise once is not the magic treatment that makes my existential fear completely vanish. But it does give me a tool for using my underlying existential fear to appreciate life, if only for a few minutes. To stay on track I need to repeat this from time to time, especially when I'm having a bad day.

And according to researchers, these types of gratitude exercises seem to have positive effects. Research done at the University of California indicated that writing in a gratitude journal once a week boosts levels of happiness. Another study found that gratitude exercises also improve physical health, raise energy levels, and relieve pain and fatigue in patients with neuromuscular disease.

When we cultivate our appreciation for life, certain things happen. We understand what is truly important and feel committed to make the most of every moment. We also experience a strong sense of compassion for all other beings as well as ourselves. And paradoxically, our existential fear lessens because we have accepted the inevitable (that we are powerless over certain things, and that we will all die) and stopped expending energy trying to control the uncontrollable. For example, when Albert learned to understand and redirect his existential fears towards valuing what he had been so afraid of losing, he not only felt more alive than ever before but also far more appreciative of the important people in his life.

## This Moment Is All We Have

"Will I ever get better?" was the question most on my mind during my 18-month bout with Chronic Fatigue Syndrome (CFS) in my late 20s. The illness was debilitating. Most days I didn't even have the physical strength to walk around the block. I had to quit my job and school, and had very little social life, never knowing if I'd have the energy to even carry on a conversation. I was plagued by fears that I would never be cured, and that I would die desolate and alone. Here were existential fears that actually had a basis in reality. For all I knew, I might never be cured, or my condition could get worse. And at the time I felt like I was powerless to do anything about it.

One day I was sitting on the front lawn, mired in this angst, when a new thought crossed my mind. This new thought said, "But this is a good moment." And suddenly all the other thoughts stopped and I realized, "Yes, this is a good moment, and I can choose to suffer in it, or I can choose to enjoy it. That much is up to me."

From then on, part of the way I coped with my illness was to look for those moments I could enjoy, appreciating and savoring them. Seeing the sun through the trees, having a bath, listening to music— moments like these became my lifeline. I was able to use my existential fear to appreciate every small gift life had to offer.

Before this epiphany, my identity had been "powerless sick guy waiting for someone or something to heal him." And let's face it, there is not a lot of self-esteem to be derived from that kind of victim status. But choosing to live in the moment gave my life new meaning, and living a meaningful life renewed my self-esteem.

Let me be honest. This new model for managing existential fear didn't cure me of my illness or my fears. It wasn't the magic bullet. There were still lots of times I felt terrified, powerless, ill, worried about the future, and definitely not in the moment. But "powerless sick guy waiting for someone or something to heal him" was no longer the *whole* of my identity. I was now also someone who in some moments could experience profound happiness.

# IO

## A HAPPY NEUROTIC HEALING JOURNEY

### Dancing into Health

In the end, I was fortunate enough to overcome my CFS. It disappeared forever after I attended a 10-day workshop on spirituality. *What?* you ask. Haven't I been slamming New Age thought throughout this book? Yes I have. But if you read on, you'll see how my experience was far different from the quick-fix New Age "cures" that I delight in skewering. As a matter of fact, this chapter explains how the whole issue of spirituality and healing is far more complex than much of New Age thought makes it out to be.

When I look back on day one of the workshop, things had looked pretty hopeless. When I finally got to the seminar venue, a ranch in Bend, Oregon, I was sicker than ever. Getting up that morning at the crack of dawn, then taking three planes had wiped out what little energy I had left after months of battling my illness. Coming to this workshop had suddenly seemed like a terrible idea. I just hoped it wouldn't set my health and energy back for months.

The next day we woke at 6:00 a.m. for morning meditation. The leader put on music and began to lead us through a dance meditation. "You're sick—go lie down before this kills you!" screamed my mind. "Since this illness began you haven't had the strength to even walk around the block. There's no way you can dance. You're way too weak."

But my soul said "Dance." And for the next 10 days I danced,

143

chanted, did energy work, two days of fasting and silence, a sweat lodge, and dream work. Each time we'd begin a process requiring physical exertion, my mind said "no" and my soul said "yes." Each time I listened to my soul, the voices from my mind lost some of their intensity. Each day my body got stronger and healthier, and by the tenth day—believe it or not—I was completely cured! It was one of the most amazing experiences I've ever had. In the process, I had felt unconditional love, ecstasy, oneness—you name it.

## Not a Typical New Age Healing

Let me explain how I believe my physical healing occurred. For the duration of my illness, I had not been living in the world of day-to-day activities, which can include things like working, raising kids, and juggling finances. I'd spent most of my time alone, meditating, reading spiritual books, and sleeping. Through meditation I had worked on cultivating a state of "being in the moment," and at detaching from fear-based thoughts that took me away from that state. As I said before, though there were still many times when I felt sick and afraid, there were also times when I was able to experience peace, trust, and even joy.

In contrast to the easy, quick fix techniques of many New Age and motivational seminars that I lampoon in this book, I believe that what happened to me at the Oregon workshop was a culmination of my spiritual practices during the many months preceding it. The state of being I had created over those months was one which invited transformation, and the workshop was the final catalyst that made that transformation happen. And as a by-product of this transformational experience, my body healed. When an experience changes us so profoundly, the changes *sometimes* include healing on a physical level. I emphasize the word "sometimes," because as I've said before, there is no failure-proof formula for healing. To imply that there is can be profoundly damaging to those battling an illness. As I said in chapter six, AIDS activist David Lewis told me of many AIDS patients who'd bought into the New Age "prescription" that learning to love themselves enough would cure their illness. And since they were dying, it meant that they had failed at self-love, when in actual fact it was the self-love prescription that had failed them. Not that there's anything wrong with learning to love yourself; just don't set yourself up to fail by expecting it to cure you of a serious health condition.

## Fear Can Disappear—Under the Right Conditions

For the 10 days of the Oregon workshop, my existential fear was gone. I felt complete trust in the universe, and I was living fully in the moment. However, once the workshop was over and I was back home, the fear returned as I re-entered the world of everyday life. As a matter of fact, today I'm just as neurotic as ever. I still have all my fear of death and tragedy, maybe even more so now that I have a family to look after.

Here again my experience contradicts most, if not all, quick-fix New Age "cures." Many New Age gurus imply that if we follow their teachings, we will attain a permanent state of bliss, where we will live totally in the moment and be forever free from fear and other negative emotions like insecurity and self-doubt. However, I think that this state tends to only happen under certain circumstances. It seems very unrealistic to expect that we can achieve permanent bliss and freedom from negative emotions in our daily lives. Besides, as I've said before, fear and insecurity can be channeled into positive action.

I'm convinced that a major reason I managed to create this transformational state was because leading up to it, I was not subject to the stressful events of everyday life. I was able to effect a state of detachment because I was living a detached life, where the only responsibilities I had were to myself. Having that kind of freedom to just *be,* instead of always having to *do,* is a luxury not available to many of us. I can't imagine being able to spend hours a day meditating if I'd had three kids to raise, chores to do, and a nine-to-five job. I think that this is the reason many monks live in monasteries far away from cities and the pressures of daily living. To achieve a so-called higher consciousness, they must be removed from having to live in the world. They need to have large chunks of space and time to just "be." Similarly, we can go to a New Age retreat for two weeks and possibly experience universal love and bliss, but in most cases, this state doesn't last all that long once we're back to our everyday lives. Maybe there are people out there who can balance the demands of working and parenting while at the same time cultivating a higher consciousness, living perfectly in the moment, and never experiencing negative emotions. But I've never met anyone like that.

I also believe that an underlying fear of death and tragedy is a natural by-product of living in the world. When we have a career, a house, and family and friends we love, we naturally have an interest in maintaining what we have. It's frightening to think of getting sick and losing our house, or having someone we love die in a car accident. As I've said repeatedly, we are small, vulnerable creatures living in a big, scary world,where terrible things can happen for no reason at all. And in our daily lives, we are constantly reminded of this fact by the media and by conversations with others. Under these circumstances, I think being able to achieve a permanent state of bliss and freedom from our so-called negative emotions is highly unlikely. In other words, when we live in a scary world, it's normal to be afraid. And if we use our existential fear effectively, and not let it run out of control like Albert did, it can provide us with the motivation necessary to take care of our things, ourselves, and those we love.

Conversely, if we live a life free from these attachments and insulated from the media, we have far less to worry about. Let's say we are provided with a secluded place to live where everyone around us meditates and lives a spiritual existence, where we have no family or financial responsibilities, and where there is no access to TV, newspapers, or the Internet. Chances are far better that we will be able to transcend existential fear and perhaps achieve a higher state of consciousness. The only problem is that this free-from-attachment lifestyle isn't a realistic option for many of us. Thus the New Age "you can achieve permanent bliss and transcend negative feelings forever" message becomes a setup for failure. Though told that we should want and be able to attain this highly spiritual state of being, we live lives that make it virtually impossible to do so. Not only that, but as I've said before, negative emotions are often the key to success and happiness, so why would we want to get rid of them?

The belief that anyone can and should permanently attain this state of "perma-bliss" while living a so-called normal life is what is wrong with much of current New Age thought. As I've said earlier in this book, it creates a no-win situation. According to the authors, teachers, and seminar leaders who propagate this belief (sometimes for great financial profit), if we fail to achieve perma-bliss, it means we haven't tried hard enough, don't love ourselves enough, or are somehow choosing to sabotage ourselves. Thus, to prove our willingness to become spiritually evolved, we must admit to having these fundamental flaws and seek to eradicate them by taking the next level of our chosen leader's program.

If we fail to use our skepticism to break free from this New Age dogma, we can end up taking years of costly seminars in an attempt to achieve something that we will in all likelihood never achieve. In other words, we can spend large chunks of time and money trying to get rid of normal human emotions, and then feel guilty and inadequate when we are unable to do so. Thus, my question is this: Who really benefits from these teachings? Ourselves or our seminar leaders?

## Spiritual, or Just Self-Absorbed?

Something we Happy Neurotics need to realize is that practicing spirituality, ironically, can be counterproductive if we put too much emphasis on it in our daily lives. Though supposed to free us from the desires of our egos, it can also be a very self-absorbed way to live. A friend who is a single mother once dated a man who lived a very spiritual lifestyle. The problem was that he was so focused on doing hours of "spiritual work" each day that he resented anything (including my friend and her child) that got in the way.

My challenge to all the New Age higher-consciousness folks is this: Try taking seven four-year-olds to the amusement park for a day, and see if you can remain perfectly blissful, free of all so-called negative emotions, and perfectly in the moment. See if you can transcend any fear you have for their safety, completely trusting the universe as they run in seven different directions, demanding to go on the "big people's rides," stuffing their faces with candy, and then needing to go to the bathroom—all at different times. If you can do that, then as far as I'm concerned, you are a spiritual master. If not, maybe you should go back to meditating in a tranquil environment where there is no one present under the age of 50.

## Formula? What Formula?

When they hear my story, people sometimes ask why I don't make a career of healing those suffering from Chronic Fatigue Syndrome or other illnesses. If I found a way to do it, they say, I should be able to duplicate it for others. Just set up a retreat with lots of dancing, chanting, and meditation. Maybe I could be another big New Age guru, with people coming from all over the world to bask in my presence. Just knowing that there was someone like me who had the "formula" to heal illness would help alleviate the fears of lots of people.

Here again is where I differ with much New Age thinking. I don't believe there is such a formula. I know that I could never deliver on the promise to heal others. No one, especially me, has a magic cure or instant, easy method for spiritual enlightenment and perfect health. A widespread New Age philosophy maintains that if you have an illness it's because you don't love yourself enough, and that once you correct this deficiency, your health will return. If it were that simple, then no one would ever get sick! Whenever we felt an illness coming on, we'd just look in the mirror and say, "I love you" to ourselves, or take ourselves out for a romantic dinner, and *presto,* we'd be healed! As anyone who has been ill or supported a loved one through an illness knows, the question of why people become ill and how to cure them is far more complex.

Near the beginning of my illness, a well-intentioned friend who'd read several New Age books on healing and considered himself an expert on the subject opined, "David, you must have chosen to get sick because there was something you needed to learn." At the time, I meekly accepted his pronouncement. Looking back I wish I'd said, "Obviously, I need to learn to not listen to morons like you." I might have added, "Besides, how stupid do you think I am? If I had that much control over my life, I'd have chosen to be an outrageously healthy, rich, gorgeous genius, instead of a skinny, bald guy with an average IQ and no energy."

Not only do I not have the formula to heal others, I don't even know that I could heal myself if I got sick again. I think that my healing from CFS was partly due to me, and partly due to chance, luck, synchronicity, or whatever else people call those amazing coincidences that come along and change our lives. I put in the work meditating and reading throughout the duration of my illness, when I could have just spent 14 hours a day in front of the TV. As well, the right book or teacher kept appearing at the right moment, through what seemed at the time to be fluke coincidences, flukes that eventually led me to the workshop in Bend, Oregon. Also, it's important to note that I didn't go to the workshop to be healed. I went because what the leader had said in his books had moved me, and I wanted to experience his ideas in person. I don't know that I would have been healed had I gone there specifically for the purpose of being healed.

Thus, the idea that I could have a generic, New Age healing formula like "Just learn to love yourself" becomes absurd. How do you set up a program where sick people seeking healing do lots of unstructured meditating for about a year, then go to a 10-day workshop without expectations of being healed? And without the certainty that I can even heal myself if I get sick again, I'm left once again with all of my existential fears.

## Fear as a Teacher

While I can't offer a get-well plan, I do have some thoughts to offer to Happy Neurotics on how to productively deal with existential fears that can arise from being sick. My healing had to do with going way outside my comfort zone and doing things I'd never done before, a process that profoundly changed me forever. What motivated me to do that was definitely not a New Age belief that I should trust the universe to provide a cure. It was my good old fear of death and tragedy (remember, as I've been saying, Happy Neurotics know they can benefit from their fears). In the beginning of my illness, I tried to get cured via conventional methods. First I went to doctors who ran tests, found nothing, and then told me it was "all in my head." One doctor suggested I would be cured if I went home and "forgot all about it." Then I went to several naturopaths who had me change my diet and take hundreds of dollars' worth of vitamins and herbal supplements, all to no avail. I also tried Chinese medicine and psychic healing—with no success. I even consulted a "healing consultant," who turned out to be a distributor for a multi-level marketing brand of vitamins and supplements, some of which I'm embarrassed to say I actually bought. And when these had no effect, he recommended other products, which surprise, surprise, he also happened to distribute. After all, as he constantly reminded me, buying his products was a way of showing that I loved myself, and if I didn't love myself enough I'd never get healed. Thanks to my lack of skepticism and his constant reminders, I ended up loving myself to the tune of about $1500.

As each method failed to cure me, my fear increased, motivating me to try various New Age self-healing techniques. I began with a book of healing affirmations, which directed me to put Post-it notes all over the house that said things like, "I affirm that I am now whole and healthy." My roommate responded with a suggestion for me on a Post-it note of her own: "I now affirm myself in the privacy of my own room." I also bought CDs that took me through healing visualizations, where among other things, I pictured white energy going through my body and washing away my illness. Though I affirmed and visualized religiously, my condition did not improve.

By then I had been sick for about six months, and I was desperately afraid. I realized that even though the self-healing techniques were new and unusual to me, I was still looking for someone to give me the "magic formula." What if there *was* no formula? Now I was really terrified.

### Just Say "Yes" to Fear

As far as I'm concerned, it was at this point that my true spiritual work commenced. The shift began when an author, whose book I'd chosen on impulse, suggested that instead of saying "no" to my existential fears, I should try saying "yes." At first I didn't get it. Fear was a bad thing. Wasn't it? The New Age books I'd read up to this point said that my fear had caused my illness. If I could eliminate fear and trust the universe, I would be cured. Besides, what did it mean to say "yes" to my fear?

While I wanted to dismiss this as a ridiculous idea, something about saying "yes" to my fear also intrigued me. Besides, what did I have to lose? I was getting sick of using up all my Post-it notes. And I came to realize that the "yes" I was supposed to say did not imply that I enjoyed being afraid. Saying "yes" simply meant that I had to *accept* my fear instead of trying to *eliminate* it. That to me meant finding a way to listen to it and allow it to guide me. And in this undertaking, New Age clichés like "Trust the universe . . . Everything happens for a reason . . . Just let yourself become one with spirit," were of little help. I realized then that I'd have to make this process up as I went along.

I decided to start by changing my focus. Okay, I would accept my fears of illness and death. Instead of trying to heal myself, I made it my goal to listen to my fear. Period. But how do you listen to fear? In the end, after a lot of trial and error, I found that what worked best for me was following my breath, spending hours sitting quietly, watching it go in and out of the parts of my body where I felt my fear. Any thoughts that arose I allowed to come and go, trying my best not to engage them. This led to my first big insight: Listening to my fear actually involved allowing myself to experience it in my body. Realizing this gave me great comfort, because no matter how sick I felt, this was something I could still do. From then on, each time I felt afraid, instead of going with my thoughts, I would focus back on my breath and body.

Listening to my fear in this manner also forced me to accept the fact that, ultimately, I was alone with my illness, and that no one out there could cure me. All I could do was keep listening. And in an odd way that realization also gave me some peace. After months of going to others to get healed, I actually had something I could do myself.

## Journey without a Map

I sensed that I was going on a journey, but I didn't know to where I was going, how I would get there, or if I would *ever* get there. My only directions came from the insights generated when I listened to my fear. I realized that much of who I was prior to my illness didn't exist anymore, and that this journey would involve some sort of fundamental change. During this time, a Tarot card depicting a tower being blown to rubble by a lightning bolt caught my attention. I felt like I was the tower and the lightning bolt was my CFS. The whole structure of my life had been demolished by my illness. I saw myself in the ruins with all the broken pieces, knowing that my job was to put them back together but that they would never fit the same way as before.

Over time, more insights came. In order to put the pieces of myself together again, I comprehended that I must build a different structure. To rebuild myself in a new form I had to move towards the unknown, towards experiences that stimulated me and made me feel alive, and away from ones that deadened me. These new experiences would provide the building blocks for my new identity. Saying New Age affirmations or doing visualizations now felt stale. After all, these were others' formulas, and I felt most alive when I found my own.

Over time I developed different ways to access my life force. For several months I listened to comedy tapes each day, experiencing the laughter deep in my body before I meditated. I also learned to chant by taking a class in Pranayama meditation, and then adapted what I had learned to suit me. Interestingly, I noticed that after each class, not only did I feel more alive, I had more physical energy. I concluded that doing spiritual practices with a group had a more powerful effect on me than when I practiced on my own.

I read books by authors like Joseph Campbell, Carl Jung, John Fowles, Fritjof Capra, Thomas Mann, and Robert Pirsig, to mention just a few. What these books had in common was that they expanded my mind, making me aware of aspects of reality that were completely new to me. Some of these books had such a powerful effect that my whole body tingled for hours after putting them down.

I was no longer trying to heal myself, I was on a *journey to be alive*, and fear was my compass. All I had to do was follow it. When I did something life-affirming, my fear turned partially to excitement. When I did something deadening, my fear became repetitive, going over and over the same old thoughts, variations on the theme of "Poor me, will I ever be healed?"

And as I journeyed further into life, my physical energy level increased. I still lacked enough energy to work or go to school, but I was able to start having a bit of a social life and to also attend some lectures on topics that drew my attention. But I also felt that for the next step in my transformation I needed to go to some sort of retreat where I could experience the concentrated spiritual energy of a group over a period of several days or even weeks. And thus it was that I was drawn to the workshop in Oregon. At the time I was also considering another seminar, but my fear became my greatest excitement when I thought of going to Oregon, so I figured that was where I had to go.

## Okay, Okay, Here's a Formula — Sort Of

As you know, I came home from Oregon completely healed, and for a short time afterwards, without fear. But as I have already said, today I have all my existential fears back, and I attempt to use them as motivation to take good care of myself and those I love. But I did learn a few things about fear and healing. And my point in telling them to you is not that you should do these exact same things. Take what you like and leave the rest. My hope is that understanding the process I went through will inspire and give you the courage to follow your own.

As I've already said, if I got sick again, I don't know if I could heal myself by doing the exact same things I did before. Rather than being able to use my previous journey as a formula to fall back on, I realize now it would just be a starting point. Once again I would have to set out with no map, although I think that listening to my fear and seeing where it pulled me would be a good beginning. Similarly, asking the question, "Is this thing I'm doing now enlivening or deadening?" would probably be a good way to keep on track. By moving towards life affirming things, I would again seek to transform myself rather than heal my illness. But let me be honest. If I got CFS or some other major illness again, I know I would be just as terrified as I was the first time. I'd probably also feel sorry for myself, and curse the universe for doing this to me. And I'd also want someone to just fix me as quickly and easily as possible, and then I'd probably resent it when no one could. In all likelihood, I'd miserably bemoan my fate to anyone who would listen, doing my best to extract sympathy for my plight. It might take me months to get to the point where I even considered saying "yes" to my fear again.

And I know there's no guarantee it would work this time. At one point in his life, my friend Claude Dosdall had a brain tumor the doctors said was terminal. Claude, too, went on a journey of transformation, and his tumor disappeared. He wrote a book about his experience called *My God I Thought You'd Died.*

But 16 years later, around the time I met him, Claude's tumor had returned. This time around, Claude told me that he didn't know if he could heal himself. Eventually he realized that his journey was to live a conscious dying process rather than to physically heal himself. The last time I saw him he was in a wheelchair. And when I asked how he was, he replied with something to the effect of, "This really sucks." Even though he was committed to living a conscious dying process, he was courageous enough to abandon any noble pretenses and instead truly acknowledge the reality of his situation.

## This Is Heavy Stuff—Do I Have To Do It?

Happy Neurotics know that not everyone needs to spend hours listening to their existential fears so they can have a transformational experience. As a matter of fact, most Happy Neurotics aren't all that interested in having a transformational experience unless it's absolutely necessary. In general, they like their daily lives, and don't want to miss out on any good times. And let's face it, plumbing the depths of existential fear isn't usually a barrel of laughs.

Happy Neurotics also take this being-in-the-moment thing with a dose of reality. They know they're not supposed to *only* live in the moment. They understand that there are many moments during which they should be worried about the future and should be making plans. In addition, they realize that there are moments when they're distracted or daydreaming, and they're okay with that, too.

They also acknowledge that some moments are extremely painful, and that during those moments it makes sense to seek some sort of escape. I admit it: I hate pain. When the dentist sticks his needle in my gums, the last thing I want is to be fully present for that moment. So I do my best to get out of it by thinking about sex and how nice it would be to get some! Seriously, I will do almost anything to get out of fully experiencing the fact that a syringe is about to be inserted into one of the tenderest areas of my body. I'll distract myself by counting the dentist's nose hairs, worrying that I'll get cancer, or imagining that a giant meteor is about to strike the earth.

Happy Neurotics know it's unrealistic to expect themselves to use their existential fear to be fully present in every moment. As a matter of fact, having that expectation just creates even more fear, fear that they might miss the next moment, or that they've already missed the previous one. Instead of expecting themselves to use existential fear to experience joy in every moment, Happy Neurotics know that the trick is to use it to create *enough* moments when they fully experience the joy of being alive.

## HUMOR: A HAPPY NEUROTIC'S BEST FRIEND

### What's So Funny About Being Insecure?

Anguish dominated Susan's face as she spoke. "I hate being insecure in my relationships with men. I just hate it. I'm afraid it'll never go away."

Wracking my brain for something to say, I remembered a technique I teach in comedy class: "Tell me why you love being insecure."

Susan was taken aback: "What do you mean?"

"Complete this sentence, 'I love being insecure because. . . .'"

"I love being insecure . . . because . . . ," she said with hesitation. "I've turned it into a game where I manipulate my boyfriend by pretending I'm totally dependent on him. . . ."

I smiled encouragingly.

She thought for a moment, and I could see a light bulb turn on in her head. "I love being insecure because then he always has to do what I say and be nice to me so I don't get hurt." She started to build up steam. "I love being insecure because then I get to spend time planning new ways to manipulate my boyfriend. I love being insecure because I've gotten so good at manipulation that I can get him to do anything." A smile lit up her face. "I love being insecure because it feels great to have that much power over someone. And I'm really good at it too. I'm the best at being insecure." By now she was laughing.

"So you're a very powerful person in your insecurity."

"Yeah, I am."

"Wow, that's amazing. I'm really impressed. You're very skilled," I said.

"I know. It's bizarre. I never realized."

"So tell me why you manipulate him."

"It's so he'll immediately drop everything and tell me he loves me, and that he'll be there forever and ever and do anything I want."

"And does it work?"

"Always."

"You're awesome. What do you do to manipulate him?"

"Well, all I have to do is look at him a certain way, or use a certain tone of voice and he gets totally worried."

By this time we were both laughing.

"And sometimes when he gives in too easily, I do something else to freak him out, like pick a fight about something he did earlier, or say 'Oh fine,' but in such a way that he thinks I'm pissed off. Or my favorite is when I cry and ask him for a hug, and when he gives it to me, I tell him not to touch me."

At this point I jumped in again. "You've told me all your friends are guys. Are they attracted to you?"

"Oh yes," Susan answered looking both embarrassed and proud. "I could have any one of them. They think I'm great."

"So in your insecurity you not only have one guy who'll do anything for you, but also four or five others dying to take his place."

Now Susan was really getting it, understanding how creative and resourceful that insecure part of her was. She had gone from hopeless victim to the maker of her own destiny in about five minutes. Not to mention coming up with some really funny material should she ever want to do stand-up comedy.

And most important, in the months and weeks to come, Susan transformed from neurotic basket case to Happy Neurotic by changing the way she dealt with her insecurity. Though she still felt it, she chose to express it in ways that built self-esteem, and which ultimately decreased her insecurity. Rather than sulk or pick a fight, Susan would tell her boyfriend when she was feeling insecure and ask for appropriate feedback and support. The more she got her needs met directly, the better she felt about herself.

Seeing herself through a comedy lens defused Susan's tendency to express insecurity in an unhealthy fashion. Being able to laugh at herself freed her from years of repeating the same mistakes. In this chapter we'll look at why humor helped produce that shift, and how we too as Happy Neurotics can use humor to channel our negative emotions in ways that build self-esteem.

## How Humor Builds Self-Esteem

My wife Beatrice used to work at a welfare office on the front lines of a poor neighborhood. Her team served difficult, high-needs clients. And as if that wasn't tough enough, she had a caseload of about 300 and worked for an organization undergoing massive funding cuts, downsizing, and policy changes. Bea was trapped in a classic no-win situation, being asked to do a job that was in fact impossible to do.

Naturally she felt a combination of intense frustration, anger, despair, and anxiety. No matter how many times she told herself to relax, to not take it personally, and that she was happy, confident, and complete within herself, she still felt bad. And she felt bad about feeling bad because after all, this was just a job, not her entire world. She felt that she should be able to control what happened inside by adopting a positive attitude each and every day.

The one time she looked forward to was afternoon coffee break, when the same thing happened each day. Her supervisor and two coworkers would appear in the reception area. "What song do you wanna hear? Do you wanna hear Jazz? Rock? Folk?" they'd ask. Then, "playing" staple removers as finger cymbals and accordion folders, the whole office would launch into the world's worst rendition of "Across The Universe" by John Lennon, all the while laughing hysterically. Says Bea, "All of a sudden I would feel in control and okay about myself, which was pretty crazy when you think about it."

Maybe not. Hungarian author and humorist George Mikes says, "In lands more familiar with oppression, a joke is necessary for one's self-esteem. Laughter is the only weapon the oppressed can use against the oppressor." But sometimes the oppressor isn't a dictator; it's our feelings. When describing a situation that makes them feel bad, my clients often say, "But I don't want to feel this way." Just as in a dictatorship people feel powerless to eliminate the oppressive regime, in our lives we sometimes feel powerless to eliminate unpleasant emotions. Being unable to do so eats away at our self-esteem. Like Bea, many of us believe we're supposed to just get over things and take control. Being incapable of "moving on" leaves us with not only our initial anxiety or insecurity but also with a sense of shame. We may think, "What's wrong with me that I can't make this feeling go away?" Though she would eventually use the negative emotions her workplace evoked as motivation to find another line of work, Bea still had to cope until she left her job as a welfare worker.

In chapter four you learned that we cannot always choose how we feel, but we can choose how we respond to our feelings. Bea and her colleagues responded to their feelings of anger and despair with humor, using it to channel these emotions in ways that built self-esteem. Choosing a response that temporarily alleviated some of their negative emotions helped them feel they had some control. And taking that control made them feel better about themselves, which is what building self-esteem is all about. The fact they could make each other laugh also heightened their self-esteem.

Did humor help Bea and her colleagues completely transcend the negativity of their workplace? Did it miraculously change their attitude so nothing bothered them? Were they imbued with love, light, and compassion for the human race? No, no, and no. If you've read this far, you know there is no miracle cure, no two-minute remedy that will eliminate feelings like anger and despair. Humor was not the panacea for Bea and her coworkers, but it did make a bad situation more bearable.

Likewise for Susan, my client who hated being insecure in her relationships with men, seeing the humor in her behavior was not the instant remedy for all her problems. Just because she had had a good laugh and gained insight didn't mean she was transformed forever. Seeing humor in her behavior helped create a shift, which she then had to reinforce by making healthy choices over and over again. It was hard work, and at times she regressed, caught herself, and moved forward again. Humor was but one tool she used as part of a long and challenging journey.

## Humoring Your Unhealthy Behaviors

Nazi Germany, Stalinist Russia, and Maoist China had a very odd thing in common. They all considered humor to be such a powerful weapon, that they outlawed jokes deemed harmful to their regimes. So much for the old saying, "Sticks and stones can break my bones but names can never hurt me." Obviously, names also pack a huge punch.

In her essay "Quisling Humor in Hitler's Norway: Its Wartime Function and Postwar Legacy," humor researcher Kathleen Stokker argues that jokes directed at Norwegian Nazi leader Vidkun Quisling and the German occupiers "protected the self-respect of and granted a measure of control to a small nation caught in an uncontrollable situation."

According to Ms. Stokker, "Norwegian resisters used humor as one of their most effective weapons." Their sizeable body of anti-Quisling jokes produced an alternative view of and helped consolidate public opinion against the Nazi regime. The population desperately needed this alternative view, since the Nazis imposed strict media censorship, and all people got were glowing reports of Hitler's war efforts.

What the anti-Hitler, anti-Mao, and anti-Stalin jokes did was make these powerful leaders seem absurd and petty. And when something becomes absurd and petty, it loses much of its power over us. Humor helped Susan see the absurdity of some of her behaviors, thus their intensity weakened. Suddenly it felt ridiculous to manipulate her boyfriend by asking for a hug, and then saying, "Don't touch me." It was hard to keep a straight face when she picked a fight instead of directly stating her needs.

In the last chapter you met Albert, whose fantasy of building an impregnable fortress symbolized his sense of fear and powerlessness. Joking about his fears helped Albert see how ludicrous it was to constantly obsess over things that in all probability would never happen. Though he still did it, his catastrophizing lost some of its power, making it easier for him to spend time living in the moment, rather than always planning for future disasters.

## Using Humor To Reduce Shame and Addiction

Shame thrives in secrecy, telling us, "There's something terribly wrong with you and if people ever find out, they'll hate and reject you. Don't let anyone get a close look at who you are." Sometimes clients take a year of therapy before revealing their dreaded secret, and most of the time my reaction is the same: "That's it? I'm disappointed. I was expecting something truly appalling. I was all set to hear that you were a serial killer or something equally heinous. What you've told me may be sad or tragic," I often continue, "but you've done nothing to warrant that kind of shame. There's nothing inherently bad about you. That shame was put onto you by other people, and it's time to start getting rid of it."

Once their deep, dark secret has been brought into the light, it begins to lose its power. The fact that one person has heard it and not rejected them gives clients a sense of hope. They think, "Maybe I'm not so bad after all. Maybe people will understand." Which is where support groups come in. Disclosing our hideous secret, receiving support and acceptance, and realizing that others have had similar experiences greatly defuse our shame. Support groups help us to become Happy Neurotics by providing us with a venue where we can channel our shame in ways that build self-esteem, in this case by seeking support from the appropriate people.

Though it's not supposed to be, my Stand-Up Comedy Clinic class is a great support group. In most support groups, you tell your story while people listen in respectful silence. In Stand-Up Comedy Clinic, you tell your story while people laugh and applaud. Former student Shawn McCreight wrote this joke:

> I'm depressed, and people don't see the positive side to depression. For example, a workout for me is eating a Snickers bar then lying down and beating myself up for half an hour.

At our final showcase, students have 200 audience members laughing with them. They get feedback like: "I loved your bi-polar jokes." "That bit about getting dumped was hilarious!" Joking about their

162

flaws and eliciting positive feedback makes students feel accepted for who they are. They have used humor to channel their shame in ways that build self-esteem. As one of them told me, "This class made me realize that we're all screwed up, that we all get through, and that we're all okay."

A stand-up comedy course that I taught to a group of addicts in a three-month residential recovery house program had a similar effect. We met once a week for eight weeks, developing comedy acts about drugs, addictions, and the experience of being in recovery. Here are some jokes they wrote:

> There are three great things about going on a date with another addict: The food bill is never too high because no one eats. It's always romantic—you sit in candlelight because there's no hydro. And you know you're safe because you always have the cops following you.

> At the Recovery House all of us live together, and the great thing about living with 15 other addicts is I don't need to watch my stuff 'cause it's already gone.

> The best thing about living with 15 other addicts is telling stories about when you sold some guy baking soda instead of cocaine. And the worst thing about living with 15 other addicts is having to room with the guy you sold it to.

There were 15 people in the program. Six wanted to perform, writing their acts with help from the entire group. Needless to say, the audience of 150 friends, family, and recovering addicts loved the show. It was incredibly inspiring to see people who five months ago had been living on the street, in skid row hotels, or in jail, get onstage and tell their stories with humor. Or to put it in Happy Neurotic terms, it was great to see them use humor to channel their shame in ways that built self-esteem.

Interestingly, the nine non-performers all relapsed almost immediately after the recovery house program ended. Of the six performers, two relapsed, and the rest were still clean several years later. The leader of the recovery house program expressed surprise that comedy seemed to have such a profound effect. As far as he was concerned, speaking their truth while 150 people laughed with and applauded them changed how performers felt about themselves. The huge hit of validation helped them accept themselves, flaws and all—at least for now.

I've also seen similar changes take place in students who take Stand Up for Mental Health, the program where I teach stand-up comedy to people with mental illness as a way for them to build confidence and fight public stigma. Through doing comedy, people rediscover a part of themselves that is strong and resilient. By finding the humor in their pain, they tap into one of their internal resources that in many cases is the reason they're still alive. In the mental health field, a major trend is "strength-based work," which involves tapping into client's strengths rather than focusing entirely on what's wrong with them. As far as I'm concerned, a sense of humour is one of the greatest strengths any of us has.

Jessica, one of my Stand Up for Mental Health students, had a long history of dealing with schizophrenia. Though very talented and bright, she always felt very ashamed of having a mental illness. This shame made it especially hard for her to ride the bus. She would sit there feeling like a social outcast, sure that everyone else was judging her. While taking Stand Up for Mental Health, she rediscovered her sense of humor and realized that she could make others laugh. One day she got on a bus and cracked jokes with some of the other riders. For her, this was a huge breakthrough. All of a sudden she felt like she had the skills to connect with and bring joy to others. For the first time in years she felt worthwhile. Jessica also experienced other changes. After a few weeks of class she showed up wearing a striped shirt, something the voices in her head had not allowed her to do for years. She explained that though the voices were still there, developing her sense of humor seemed to have in some cases lessened their intensity.

As I keep repeating—there is no miracle cure. Laughter will not make someone's schizophrenia vanish. But it does seem to make it easier to cope. Also, change takes place over time and requires constant reinforcement. For comedy to achieve a truly lasting impact, I believe the performers need to do shows on an ongoing basis. It's not enough to just get one hit of comedy validation and acceptance from an audience. It's by having this experience over and over again that the comics really start to change. We often need a lot of positive feedback to begin to shift a negative self-image that's been there for years. That's why Stand Up for Mental Health is an ongoing program.

## You Don't Need To Do Stand-Up Comedy

Not everyone wants to do stand-up comedy. And the good news is that you don't have to. Almost anyone can take steps towards becoming a Happy Neurotic by using humor to channel negative emotions in ways that build self-worth. Take Albert. One of the principles of humor is that to see the absurdity in a situation, you must grossly exaggerate your thoughts, fears, and behaviors. Thus, we resolved that, instead of attempting to lessen his fears, Albert would now exaggerate them. For example, instead of saying to his wife, "I have a plugged nose, I think I might be getting the flu," he would say, "I've got a plugged nose—I must be getting cancer." Or instead of, "I'm concerned about that strange car parked out front," he would say, "I'm sure that strange car parked out front means we'll be invaded by a gang of crackheads tonight."

His wife would respond with something like, "Let's rush you to the emergency ward right away," or "Yes, I'm sure the crackheads will invade after dinner."

The couple would laugh, and Albert would realize how absurd his fear was, and feel proud of being able to defuse it with humor.

Susan's use of humor was similar. Instead of hiding her insecurity by picking a fight with her boyfriend, she would exaggerate it, making a joke like, "I need reassurance that you love me. I want you to sing my praises non-stop for the next 12 hours. But before you start, let me get my MP3 player so I can record you." Her boyfriend would laugh, pretend to get an MP3 player and mime into a microphone, "You're the greatest" over and over. Susan would feel good she had made her boyfriend laugh and gotten reassurance in a positive way. What used to be a painful ordeal for both of them was now quickly defused.

According to psychoanalyst Harvey Mindess, "The very act of making fun of our inferior position raises us above it." By joking about our insecurity, anxiety, and fear, we create an inverse superiority. Others may surpass us, but we're better at being inferior. Instead of feeling ashamed, Susan now took pride in her insecurity, since when it came to being insecure, she was the best!

Or take me. Brad Pitt may be more successful and attractive, but I'm better at being a geek. Anthony Robbins may be more positive and self-assured, but I'm better at whining and complaining.

Another comedy student based her act on how tough it was to get a date as a single mother. She wrote this joke:

> Yesterday my son brought a flyer home from school. It said, "Safety Alert! A teacher on her lunch break observed a naked man in the parking lot, approximately age 30, height six feet, slim build."
>
> He's a little young but I think I'll go for it.
>
> Not only did she get a huge laugh, but after the show a man in the audience gave her his phone number and said, "Call me—I'd love to go on a date!" Talk about positive validation!

## Without Your Inferiority, You'd Be Nothing

We all have aspects of ourselves we don't like. Maybe we get nervous at parties, can't get a date, procrastinate, get overly emotional, or are terrified of spiders. According to the myth of perfection, we should eliminate these flaws. Let's pretend for a moment that was possible. Let's pretend we could be perfect in every way. If that were the case, we'd lose one of our most precious resources—self-deprecating humor.

In comedy class I tell students: "Your act is your pain. People want to hear about your struggles, because then they can identify with you. You become one of them. No one wants to hear about how perfect you are. No one wants to hear that you're happy and well adjusted. And if by some incredible fluke you are perfect, then you'd better create some problems. In comedy your weaknesses are your strengths."

The same goes for humor in everyday life. Self-deprecating humor endears us to others, building bridges and creating bonds. The more flaws we have, the more self-deprecating humor we can use. Often it is not our strengths but our vulnerabilities that make it safe for others to approach. Though told we must strive for perfection, we might not ever feel comfortable around someone who was perfect, until we saw that she too had vulnerabilities.

## Self-Deprecating Humor Skills for the Happy Neurotic

No one seems to be able to explain how to come up with self-deprecating humor. People say things like: "Don't take yourself so seriously." "See the funny side of your problems." "When life gives you lemons, make lemonade." But it's difficult to turn these generalities into specific behaviors. How do you not take yourself so seriously? By seeing the funny side! But how do you see the funny side? By making lemonade?

To use humor or to make any kind of changes in their life, people need specifics. Telling Bill to resolve a conflict in his relationship is a start, but "resolving a conflict" is vague and means different things to different people. To achieve success, Bill needs to define exactly what he's attempting to do, and what the steps are to do it. And it's the same with humor. Telling Susan to lighten up about her insecurity is fine, but to succeed, she needs to know exactly how to do that.

Humor involves two main components: surprise and exaggeration that create laughter or elicit good feelings. Only one of these elements needs to be present, though together they pack a more powerful punch. Susan's request to have her boyfriend praise her for 12 hours into an MP3 player contained both components. She grossly exaggerated the amount of reassurance she needed, and the idea of using a tape recorder added an unexpected twist. Albert's statement "I've got a plugged nose—I think I'm getting cancer" contained both an exaggeration of his fear and a surprise conclusion because we normally wouldn't think of a plugged nose leading to cancer.

## How To Prepare Spontaneous Self-Deprecating Humor

Many people think that humor can only occur spontaneously. They may say, "My humor is totally off the cuff. I can't plan it. It just happens." Of course, spontaneous humor is wonderful. But the problem is waiting for it to occur, and let's face it: the inspiration isn't always there, especially when we most need it. It's those times when we feel tongue-tied, nervous, embarrassed, or afraid, that our relaxed, impromptu wit vanishes.

The belief that humor only arises spontaneously also stems from a misconception about stand-up comedy. People think that comics are able to walk onstage and be spontaneously funny for an hour. Nothing could be further from the truth. Stand-up comedy is about 80 percent written and rehearsed and 20 percent spontaneously ad-libbed. If you watch a comic two nights in a row, you'll pretty much see the same show. You'll realize that even some of those ad-libs that appeared spontaneous and brilliant are a planned part of the routine. Also, why do you think comics almost always win battles with hecklers? True, comics have the microphone, but they also have "canned" heckler lines. One of the ones you may have heard is, "C'mon sir, I don't come to your job and criticize you."

We too can prepare spontaneous humor. And unless we want to use it as stand-up comedy, our prepared humor doesn't need to be night club funny. When we pay to see a comic, expectations are high that she will make us laugh. The expectations are much lower in everyday conversation, so laughs are much easier to come by. Studies of laughter in everyday conversation find that only 10–20 percent of laughter is in response to something humorous. The other 80–90 percent is used for social purposes like filling pauses or conveying agreement, empathy, and support for the speaker. In other words, you have an 80–90 percent chance of getting laughs if others like you, whether or not you are actually funny!

And don't forget to apply the Happy Neurotic success formula—setting your expectations so low you'll never be disappointed. Instead of expecting a huge laugh, go for a smile, a chuckle, or any sign of life! Or maybe at first, decide that just saying one joke or a witty one-liner is a success, regardless of the response you get. And once you've told a joke once, you can try for a stronger delivery the second time, gradually raising the bar each time you tell it.

Here are some formulas that provide strategies for preparing spontaneous self-deprecating humor:

## The "I Don't" Formula

To communicate your fears in a humorous way, complete the following three-part sentence. The sentence contains your fear, a logical thing you need from others or must do yourself to alleviate it, and then a grossly exaggerated one. Here's what the sentence and the result look like:

"To _____, I don't just _____, I need _____."

"To *lessen my fear of abandonment, I don't just need you to tell me you'll be faithful, I need you to put your house up as collateral!*"

Here are the steps to get there:

**Step One:** Identify a fear you have.

"*I'm afraid of abandonment.*"

**Step Two:** Now write down a relatively normal thing you need from others or must do yourself to diminish this fear.

"To *lessen my fear of abandonment, I don't just need you to tell me you'll be faithful,*"

**Step Three:** Now come up with something way more exaggerated that you need from others or must do yourself to lessen this fear.

"To *lessen my fear of abandonment, I don't just need you to tell me you'll be faithful, I need you to put your house up as collateral!*"

Here's another example:

**Step One:** Identify a fear you have.

"*I'm afraid of getting sick.*"

**Step Two:** Write down a relatively normal thing you need from others or must do yourself to diminish this fear.

"To *lessen my fear of getting sick, I don't just wash hands after using a public phone,*"

**Step Three:** Now come up with something way more exaggerated that you need from others or must do yourself to lessen this fear.

"To lessen my fear *of getting sick, I don't just wash hands after using a public phone, I disinfect my whole body!*"

Here is a blank template you can use.

**Step One:** Identify a fear you have.

*"I'm afraid* _____*,*

**Step Two:** Now write down a relatively normal thing you need from others or must do yourself to diminish this fear.

*"To* _____*, I don't just need*

_____*"*

**Step Three:** Now come up with something way more exaggerated you need from others or must do yourself to lessen this fear.

*"To* _____*, I don't just need*

_____*, I need*

_____*."*

Feel free to alter this formula as you see fit. For example, instead of always saying, "To lessen my fear of . . ." you could say, "To make sure people aren't talking behind my back . . ." or "To know that I've done a good job . . ."

## The "Just Makes Me" Formula

Here is another good method for creating spontaneous self-deprecating humor. Start with something that evokes a negative emotion, then exaggerate your reaction. In chapter two you met Mary, whose constant questioning of her husband's fidelity almost ruined her marriage. In both the template and finished version examples, here's something Mary would say to poke fun at herself:

*"Just* _____ *makes*

*me* _____*."*

*"Just seeing you talk to another woman makes me want to yell, 'Don't touch him! He's mine.'"*

Here are the steps to get there:

**Step One:** Identify something that evokes a negative emotion. Example: *"Blind dates"*

**Step Two:** Phrase your sentence as though you were just thinking about it or seeing it, not actually doing it. By distancing yourself from that actual thing, the exaggerated reaction you're about to add becomes even more disproportionate.

*"Just <u>thinking about a blind date</u>"*

**Step Three:** Now come up with a grossly exaggerated reaction to the thing you identified in Step One.

An exaggerated reaction to *<u>blind dates</u>* would be: *<u>Having a panic attack.</u>*

**Step Four:** Now complete the sentence by adding the exaggerated reaction from Step Three.

*"Just <u>thinking about a blind date</u> makes me <u>go into a full blown panic attack.</u>"*

Here's another example:

**Step One:** Identify something that evokes a negative emotion.

*"<u>Going to a party where I don't know anyone.</u>"*

**Step Two:** Phrase your sentence as though you were just thinking about it or seeing it, not actually doing it.

*"Just <u>thinking about going to a party where I don't know anyone</u>"*

**Step Three:** Now come up with a grossly exaggerated reaction to the thing you identified in Step One.

A grossly exaggerated reaction to *"<u>going to a party where I don't know anyone</u>"* would be: *"<u>wanting to call my trauma counselor.</u>"*

**Step Four:** Now complete the sentence by adding the exaggerated reaction from Step Three.

*"Just <u>thinking about going to a party where I don't know anyone</u> makes me <u>want to call my trauma counselor.</u>"*

Here's a template for you to use:

**Step One:** Identify something that evokes a negative emotion.

"_____"

**Step Two:** Phrase your sentence as though you were just thinking about it or seeing it, not actually doing it.

*"Just thinking about* _____"

**Step Three:** Now come up with a grossly exaggerated reaction to the thing you identified in Step One.

*An exaggerated reaction to "*_____*" would be:*

"_____"

**Step Four:** Now complete the sentence by adding the exaggerated reaction from Step Three.

*"Just thinking about_____ makes me*
_____."

### Shortcut:

You may not need to do Steps One to Three, just start at Step Four. If you'd like to take that shortcut, here it is:

*"Just thinking about_____ makes me*
_____."

After some practice, you'll be able to use this formula spontaneously.

## Reverse Bragging

Another way of developing self-deprecating humor is to brag about your dysfunctions. I call this "Reverse Bragging." Some of our stress can come from fearing that others will find out we're flawed and think less of us. Boasting about our flaws robs them of the chance to disapprove, since joining in the laughter puts them on our side. And letting others know we're aware of our flaws makes it harder for them to criticize us, since we've anticipated what they might say.

So what flaws do you have to brag about? What dysfunctional thing can you do better than anyone else? Are you good at catastrophizing, worrying, doubting yourself, or people-pleasing? With Reverse Bragging, these are now your strengths! Here are some techniques to help you put all this into practice:

## Reverse Bragging Technique #1:

When you hear someone talking about how good he or another person is at something, you respond with "_____ may be good at _____, but I'm way better at _____." Then describe what you do that makes you so good at this thing you've just reverse bragged about. Here's how this can sound:

**Coworker:** *"Brad has such a positive attitude, he's so great to work with."*

**You:** *"Sure Brad has a good attitude, but I'm way better at complaining and being annoying. Last night my wife asked me to take out the garbage, and I whined for at least an hour before I did it. I bet Brad couldn't do that!"*

172

Here's another example:

**Coworker:** "*Jill is so organized and efficient. I don't know what we'd do without her.*"

**You:** "*Jill may be organized, but I'm way better at screwing up and losing things. I lost my car for a week until I realized it was parked in front of my house!*"

### Reverse Bragging Technique #2

This formula is also based on the idea that our dysfunctions make us special. All we need to do is figure out how and then brag about it! To do so, merely ask these three Reverse Bragging Questions and turn the answers into Reverse Brags.

1. What does your dysfunction help you avoid?
2. What skills has it helped you develop?
3. How does it make you better than others?

Let's say you're insecure. If you ask the Reverse Bragging Questions regarding your insecurity, it might go like this:

1. What does my insecurity help me avoid?

**Answer:** "*It helps me avoid saying anything that will antagonize anyone.*"

**Reverse Brag:** "*I'm so careful about what I say that I haven't antagonized anyone since 1962! I was politically correct before it was even invented.*"

2. What skills has my insecurity helped me develop?

**Answer:** "*I'm great at intuiting where people are at and telling them exactly what they want to hear.*"

**Reverse Brag:** "*I am awesome at telling people exactly what they want to hear. As a matter of fact I tell them things they don't even know they want to hear.*"

3. How does being insecure make me better than others?

**Answer:** "*It makes me one of the most sensitive people on the planet.*"

**Reverse Brag:** "*I'm so sensitive that I know when people I've never even met are talking behind my back.*"

You can use these techniques to come up with Reverse Brags of your own, or if it's appropriate, you can use one of the above examples. You'll notice they all contain lots of exaggeration. The more you exaggerate your Reverse Bragging, the funnier it will be.

## How To Get Even More Yuks Out of Your Dysfunction

This next technique helps you find even more humor in your dysfunction. Though you can do it on your own, it works even better if you do it with a friend or support group. To begin with, you'll choose a dysfunctional part of yourself to focus on, and then plan your perfect dysfunctional day.

**Step One:** Identify a flaw or dysfunction, like being insecure, constantly worrying, or being anxiety-ridden, that you'd like to find humor in. Then add a situation or thing that seems to aggravate this trait. For example you could choose, "Being insecure around people," or "Constantly worrying about my health." Now put the two together for your complete answer. For example:

Flaw I'd like to see humor in: being insecure

Situation or thing that aggravates this trait: people

Complete answer: being insecure around people

**Step Two:** Now take a contrary attitude. This part is crucial. When thinking about these flaws we usually have an attitude of "I hate this." However, in this step I want you to take the attitude of "I love this." Many comics use this technique to help them see humor in a situation.

On a piece of paper write "I love _____ because . . ." and fill in the blank with your character flaw from Step One. This exercise tends to work best when you focus on one flaw at a time. Now number from 1 to 10 underneath your opening statement. It should look like this:

I love *being insecure around people* because:

1.

2.

3.

etc.

174

Now set a timer and give yourself five minutes to come up with 10 reasons why you love your flaw. The time factor is very important. As you do this, don't think or analyze. Just write down the first things that come to mind. Analyzing or thinking gets you tangled up in your head, making it hard to come up with anything. And don't worry about being funny, just do the exercise. This is what I came up with:

I love being *insecure around people* because:

1. I get to spend hours obsessing about whether or not they like me.
2. I get to stress myself out worrying about what they're saying behind my back.
3. I get to drive my friends and family nuts.
4. I've developed my intuition to the point where I can find other, more insecure people and manipulate them into validating me.
5. It distracts me from worrying about something real.
6. It gives me something to overcome, and that makes me better than confident people with stable personalities.
7. It gives me a reason to go to therapy.
8. It makes me special. No one is as complex and insecure as I am.
9. I've perfected the art of people-pleasing.
10. I'd be nothing without my emotional problems.

If you're having trouble coming up with your 10 reasons, use the Reverse Bragging questions to help you:

1. What do you get from your dysfunction?
2. What does it help you avoid?
3. What special skills has it helped you develop?
4. How does it make you better than other people?

## Step Three: Planning Your Perfect Dysfunctional Day

In this part of the exercise, you're going to plan your perfect dysfunctional day using the 10 reasons from Step Two. You're going to write an agenda, scheduling time to incorporate most of the 10 reasons into your daily activities. Or you can plan basic activities like coffee with a friend or a walk in the park and plan to do them as dysfunctionally as possible. It helps to include as much specific detail as possible. Most important, frame each thing in a positive light, using words indicating how much pleasure you will derive from it. Obviously, you're not going to actually do any of this stuff in real life. The idea is to find the absurdity in your dysfunction, thereby lessening its power. To give a better sense of how this works, I've included the original neurotic behavior from Step Two in brackets after each activity on my agenda.

### My Perfect Dysfunctional Day

**9:00 a.m.:** Enjoy starting the day by obsessing about whether or not the people I sat next to at dinner last night liked me. Delight in analyzing their every movement, sound, and facial gesture for signs of disapproval and contempt. (#1: Obsessing about whether people like me.)

**10:00 a.m.:** Having joyfully come to the conclusion they hated my guts, I eagerly plunge into the next activity, freaking myself out over the nasty things they're saying behind my back while I quickly choke down breakfast. (#2: Stress out by worrying about what people say about me.)

**10:30 a.m.:** Enthusiastically wallow in neurosis for the next hour, otherwise known as weekly appointment with therapist. (#7: Go to therapy.)

**11:30 a.m.:** Excitedly rush home to call wife at work in order to rehash every painful detail of therapy session. Feel hurt and betrayed when fire alarm goes off and she hangs up to join coworkers in evacuating building. (#3: Drive people nuts.)

**2:30 p.m.:** Still feel badly after call with wife. Happily console myself with thought that I'm a better person than she because I have something to overcome and she doesn't. (#6: I'm better than confident people.)

**3:00 p.m.:** Meet Fred for coffee. Fred is more insecure than I am, so I spend a pleasurable hour manipulating him into agreeing that I'm a better person than he is. (#4: Manipulate insecure people into validating me.)

**4:00 p.m.:** Go for walk in park. Many people jog past. I begin to feel inadequate but gleefully remind myself that their devotion to fitness means they are shallow conformists, whereas my complex and neurotic personality makes me unique and precious. (#8: My insecurity makes me special.)

**5:00 p.m.:** Stop at market to buy groceries for dinner. Rejoice in my ability to smile and apologize as rude shoppers with more than nine items in the express line push me aside. (#9: People-pleasing.)

Now you try. Remember that the more practiced you become at seeing the humor in your dysfunctions, the more natural it will become to catch yourself in the act and do something else. Like learning any new skill, this takes time and repetition.

## A Dose of Modern Alchemy

In medieval times, alchemists searched for the philosopher's stone, a mysterious substance that they believed had the power to transform base metals into gold. As Happy Neurotics, humor is our philosopher's stone. With it, we transform baser emotions like fear, anger, and insecurity into comedy gold. And like my Stand Up for Mental Health students, we use this gold to build our self-esteem, free ourselves from unhealthy behaviors, and create connections with the people in our world. And we give thanks for the fact that we will always have baser emotions, because it means that we will never run out of the raw material we need to create our comedy gold.

## CONCLUSION: THE FINAL CALL TO INACTION

### It's All About Being Ordinary

I love the way many books on self-help and spirituality end with an inspiring message. I finish those books feeling uplifted, revitalized, and ready to take on the world.

I sure wish my book ended that way. But all along I've been telling you that there's no magic bullet or miracle cure, that no matter how much personal growth or spiritual work you do, you'll always have negative feelings like fear, insecurity, and embarrassment. So when it comes to an inspiring ending, I've kind of shot myself in the foot. At this point, you wouldn't believe me if I said that you will achieve a state of grace, reverse the aging process, and manifest a huge fortune if you do everything I say.

The truth is that most Happy Neurotics live pretty ordinary lives. Like everyone else, they work, pay their bills, do the laundry, fall in love, and raise families. If you had them as friends you would experience them as warm, personable, and fun to be with. As you got to know them better you would see them deal with their insecurities in a straightforward, unremarkable way. If they were feeling anxious about something they would say so, and perhaps ask for feedback or support. If they had a problem, they would seek help from the appropriate people. There would be few big emotional crises in their lives, and those that occurred would in general not be the result of destructive or self-sabotaging behavior on their part.

## Why They Don't Make Movies about Happy Neurotics in Love

If you were to watch a movie about two Happy Neurotics in a relationship, you would probably lose interest quite quickly, because nothing too exciting would seem to happen. There would be no dramatic fights or heart-wrenching betrayals. Instead, you would see two people who really appreciated each other and got along well most of the time. You would see two people in love, a very ordinary, everyday love, where despite the occasional argument, the way they felt about each other never really changed.

On a day-to-day basis, you would see them "checking in" with each other about how they were feeling, discussing their fears, insecurities, joys, and hopes. In general, the most dramatic it would ever get is when they would quarrel about mundane things, like whose turn it was to cook dinner or take out the garbage. Occasionally there would be times when they were cranky or irritable. And when in conflict, they would state their point directly, instead of using sarcastic put-downs, withdrawing into hostile silence, or getting drunk. They would also listen to and respect each other's opinion, even if they didn't agree with it.

## The Happy Neurotic Family

Happy Neurotic families are also pretty ordinary. For the most part, there are no horrible fights or screaming matches, because parents encourage kids to express all of their feelings, positive or negative, in appropriate ways. Because their feelings are respected, the kids feel safe to disagree with their parents, knowing they will not always get their way but that their opinions will be listened to. Thus, the family is able to resolve conflicts, rather than allowing them to fester and turn into ticking time bombs. And when the parents discipline their kids, they do it fairly, without hitting or verbal abuse.

On the whole, Happy Neurotic parents are aware of their own fears and insecurities, and do their best not to dump them onto their kids. Let's say a parent is worried about losing his job. He will look to the appropriate adults for support, instead of burdening the kids with all his worries. He may choose to tell the kids he's concerned about his job but without going into great detail and putting them in the position of having to meet his adult emotional needs. Happy Neurotic parents realize that they are there to meet their kids' needs, not the other way around.

But Happy Neurotic families are far from perfect. They have their share of turmoil. Sometimes the kids are whiny and unreasonable, not wanting to go to bed on time, clean their rooms, or turn off the TV. Sometimes the parents are impatient and grouchy with the kids. They may administer too many time-outs or become unreasonably stubborn over small things like TV time or household chores.

As the kids go through high school, they deal with the same issues all teenagers face—drugs, sex, peer pressure, academic challenges, and the like. And they make their share of mistakes, at times frustrating their parents to no end. Raising kids to be Happy Neurotics doesn't guarantee that everything will always go smoothly. But it can help. Because kids in Happy Neurotic families have been brought up feeling safe to express themselves and knowing that their parents will listen, there is a better chance that they will work with their parents to solve whatever problems come up.

The kids in Happy Neurotic families don't always get everything they need emotionally in every moment, but over time, they get *enough* of what they need. The same goes for Happy Neurotic parents. They may not always be able to be there for each other, but they are there enough of the time. Realizing that one person can't meet all of their emotional needs, they also look to friends, support networks, extended family, and the like. Happy Neurotic parents who are single are equally aware that they must create social support networks for themselves. And with kids and parents getting enough emotional support there is less tension, so family life is reasonably smooth much of the time.

That doesn't mean life is boring. Everyone in the family has their interests and passions that they share with each other. There is lots of fun and laughter. There are lots of great conversations. It's just that there is little drama of the kind we see in movies and TV shows, where many plots depict and sometimes glamorize dysfunctional families and the unhealthy ways that the people in them interrelate.

## But What about Transformation and All that Spiritual Stuff?

As I describe how ordinary most Happy Neurotics are, you may be wondering, "What about all the stuff this author has been through? Getting a serious illness, meditating for hours and hours, then having a transformational experience is far from ordinary. Do I have to do something extraordinary like that to become a Happy Neurotic?"

The answer to your question is no. Chances are you only need to do something extraordinary if you find yourself in extraordinary circumstances. I did all that spiritual searching because I felt I had to. Had I not become ill, I doubt that I would have had the time or inclination to take that path. In chapter four I describe the hero's journey, and how when the call comes to undertake it, many of us don't want to answer. My call was the CFS, and for the longest time I didn't want to pick up the phone. I eventually did because nobody could cure me, and because I had realized that watching 14 hours a day of TV was a form of torture that no one should inflict upon himself.

As I've said repeatedly, a Happy Neurotic is someone who accepts and works with his negative emotions to channel them in positive ways that build self-esteem. In general, it is only in crisis situations that we have to go to extraordinary lengths to do that. If we're anxious about our bank account being overdrawn, we can use our anxiety as motivation to check the balance, figure out how much money is left, what to do with it, and perhaps design a budget to prevent future financial problems. Once we've taken these steps, we will presumably feel good about how we've handled this situation. By using anxiety as motivation for taking these commonplace measures, we have channeled it in a positive way that builds self-esteem without having to go to extraordinary lengths to do so.

However, let's say that someone we love suddenly dies. There is a good chance that to productively channel the negative emotions evoked by this situation requires far more extraordinary measures. Simply put, the death of a loved one generates emotions of a much greater intensity than those we normally feel on a daily basis. And in general, the more intense the emotion, the greater the efforts we must make to channel it productively. Take Mavis, the accidental comic from chapter one. She sought grief counseling and spent hours soul-searching to cope with the pain of her daughter's death. In addition, she took a stand-up comedy course (albeit by accident!) that helped her to channel the negative emotions from her situation in ways that built her self-esteem. Similarly, having CFS engendered strong feelings in me—I was terrified. More ordinary measures like thinking positively or going to the doctor, which might have been effective in less extreme circumstances, were of little help when it came to productively channeling my fear. To do that, I was forced to take measures far beyond anything I'd ever done before.

Though I learned many valuable lessons during my healing journey, I certainly didn't need it to become a Happy Neurotic. As a matter of fact, given a choice, I would've gladly skipped the whole thing. But looking back, I realize that I was a Happy Neurotic well before getting ill, and continued to be one despite my illness. I just wish I had known it at the time! That way I wouldn't have spent so much time and money trying to rid myself of emotions that are normal and human.

### The Final Call to Inaction

So if you want to become a Happy Neurotic, remember that you have it in you to achieve this very ordinary state of being—if you haven't already done so.

Every morning, look at yourself in the mirror—preferably after you've woken up—and say: "I am an ordinary person, and I will have an ordinary day. Today I will achieve nothing amazing, leave no lasting legacy, and win no awards, but I will try to have one heck of a good time." I know you can do it. Start now.

Stop striving for excellence, and go for good enough.

Set your expectations low but keep your hopes high.

When faced with a challenge, remind yourself how frightened you are of blowing it, and use the energy from your fear to catastrophize and come up with contingency plans.

Don't trust the universe to provide, but instead be skeptical and ask lots of questions. If a seminar leader says, "We are all one," ask why you have to pay him.

Refuse to talk to your inner child or stand in front of a mirror and say "I love you" to your reflection.

Remind yourself that you will never be fearless or totally confident. If some enthusiastic New Ager accuses you of being fear-based say: "Of course I am, how come you're not?"

If you're depressed, consider just going for the drugs.

Have some good laughs as you plan your perfect dysfunctional day.

Remind yourself that without your inferiority, you'd be nothing.

And above all else, stop spending time and money trying to rid yourself of normal human emotions.